PIPs Speak

Essays by Previously Important People

Edited by **Sarah-Massey-Warren, Ph.D.**
and **Luellen Ramey, Ph.D.**

PIPs Speak: *Essays by Previously Important People*

Print ISBN: 979-8-35090-384-3
eBook ISBN: 979-8-35090-385-0

Edited by
Sarah Massey-Warren, Ph.D.
Luellen Ramey, Ph.D.

Cover design by Janat Horowitz

Dedicated to

all aspiring essayists

CONTENTS

Introduction

PIPs Speak: Essays by Previously Important People is a collection of stand-on-their-own creative nonfiction essays that range from 500 to 750 words from a group of thirteen writers over the age of sixty. The essays cover the gamut from reactions to current events to thoughts on family, aging, children, and dying, very much in the spirit of Montaigne. Readers see into the world of the writer and recognize similarities to their own worlds. The prose varies from lyrical to poignant, quizzical to comic, incensed to at peace, reflecting the range of emotions being human evokes.

Inspired by a 500-word essay challenge in Sarah Massey-Warren's Intergenerational Class, the thirteen essayists contributing to this collection demonstrate that communication, creativity, and community thrive regardless of age. These short essays represent five years of connection through writing to explore themes ranging from family and relationship to loss and politics, even on Zoom during the pandemic. The writers met through their participation in Intergenerational Writing, a class pioneered by Sarah Massey-Warren and Jack Williamson. The class partnered community members over sixty with college students at the University of Colorado—the only class of this kind in the country. One of the purposes of this pilot was to break down stereotypes of each of the generations and to diminish "otherizing." Although many books of essays have been published, these essays represent a fresh look at a wide variety of issues people face generally and particularly during a pandemic through the lens of individuals over sixty. No similar collection for this specific audience exists.

We have been writing short essays and reading them aloud to the group once a month for over five years. What has kept us together is a venue to express ourselves and a sense of community when we no longer have a community through full-time careers. Writing and sharing our essays sustained us through COVID as well. We trust this collection and a description of our process will inspire other writers, particularly those over sixty, to form their own groups. We see this as an antidote not only to COVID but also to the epidemic of loneliness among elders. And we believe the content of many of these essays speaks to a broader age demographic, thus breaking down the ageist generational silos.

The essayists contributing to this collection have lived full professional lives. Rejecting the common societal view of "seniors" as background rather than players in a vibrant community, our writers represent the accumulation of thoughts and reflections obtained through the need to take on creative challenges throughout life. The book will appeal to those over sixty or anyone who wants to find their own voice or seek community in isolating times. Sarah Massey-Warren uses this same essay challenge with her University of Colorado writing students, who love it and continue to write their own essays after class ends, so the content and form appeal to a range of generations. Rather than one-way communication, essayists invite the reader into conversations on different aspects of life—love, children, challenges, spirituality, rites of passage—from birth to death. Finally, the short format makes writing a challenge and an opportunity, rather than an overwhelming onus, accessible to anybody who dreams of writing.

Development of a Group

In a writing group, the conversation expands as other writers reflect on their own experiences. Our process includes exchanging drafts of essays within smaller groups the week before we meet, making changes, then reading the essays aloud to the group the following week when we meet. Although members of the group originally decided to restrict follow-up comments to the writing itself, actual conversations extend beyond to the commonality of the experience described. The process is easily transferable to any group of writers who wish to expand their writing practice beyond their private journals and computers.

Early on, the group used prompts for writing. As they continued, most chose a subject to write about without prompts.

The group has met each month for over five years. The fact that the group is still together attests to how important and inspiring a venue for creativity and expression this group has become. We have become a community of writers. We've come to know each other primarily through the content of essays. Trust is high, judgment is low, and as time has passed, members have gone deeper with their writing.

We offer this collection of essays both as a product of our time together and our connection. We also hope that it will inspire other communities to form similar groups.

Luellen Ramey
Sarah Massey-Warren

Time in a Bottle

PEGGY WALLIS

I am listening to Jim Croce sing *"Time In A Bottle."* I've always been drawn to the idea of containing time and sharing it with those you love. Unfortunately, the bottle memorialized so beautifully in song shattered when the plane that carried it crashed into the side of a mountain. Bottles are fragile things.

My granddaughter also has a bottle, filled with time as clear and untroubled as bright blue air. Her bottle is sturdy, filled with best friends, soccer games, and hikes to waterfalls. There are no cracks or leaks, and time seems endless. In her attic she has made a potion room with many bottles filled with colored liquids. The formulas are in a potion book that only she can access. Her beautiful multicolored bottles fill my eyes when we spend time together.

Later today, I will visit my mother, who lives in a "memory care" facility. Until recently, she believed that her time was endless, an infinity of moments in a bottle that would never leak or break. But time came for her as well, and a cerebral hemorrhage cracked the smooth surface of lavender glass. Now she sits with no time at all, speaking words that I cannot understand. I visit her in her eternal present, with past and future erased. The other residents have their own bottles, more or less full, but all becoming empty. I look at their faces, some agitated and some serene, and think about time. When I look at my hands, they are the hands of my mother.

My own bottle is still filled with children, grandchildren, friends, and love. It feels full, but tiny cracks are starting to show. The days, which seemed so long when I was a child, now fly by. I want to catch them and hold on. But they elude me, wisps of shining light just beyond my grasp. I try to keep a firm grip on the present, but look to the future as well—the breathless end of a long hike.

One day, my fragile bottle, this precious time, will break in my hand sending jagged pieces of colored glass flying across the room. When that day comes, I hope that these shining fragments of glass reflect back the radiance of a life well lived and filled with love. And in these splintered shards, may my loved ones see some of me reflected, along with their beautiful faces.

Should I Stay or Should I Go?

SARAH MASSEY-WARREN

The ability to halt a line of abstract thinking once you see it has
no end is part of what usually distinguishes sane, functional
people—people who when the alarm goes off can hit the floor
without trepidation and plunge into the concrete business of the
workaday world—from the unhinged.

—David Foster Wallace

If you drive northeast on I-76 in Colorado as it curves into I-80, you notice a sign on the right. A cheerful sunrise announces, "Nebraska: The Good Life." A look in the rearview mirror reveals an ugly brown-and-white sign, twenty-five yards back, proclaiming, "Welcome to Colorful Colorado," colorful no doubt because no helmet law in Colorado protects motorcyclists. In that interim space between signs, you flail—not colorful, not the good life. Later, a bridge crosses I-80 near Paxton. On one side, a sign reads "Mountain Time;" on the other, "Central Time." The bridge lies in the Twilight Zone.

For over a decade, I have assigned my students "place essays," in which they must evoke a place without saying the word "place," and narrate that spatial concept in storytelling. Place, I tell them, exists in your head, not on the ground—out there is only space. Humans define political, social, and psychological boundaries. Things get screwier when one accounts for changes in location over time—is it the same place?

Reading David Foster Wallace's (DFW) *Everything and More: A compact theory of infinity* makes my head explode. Tracing mathematical theory about infinity over hundreds of years in his pyrotechnic prose, DFW completely obliterates all sense of place—one can't even admit to points on a line, let alone motion, which only exist in theory. DFW enumerates the brilliant math theorists who have literally driven themselves crazy, having moved infinity further into provable abstractions and complex equations.

Why am I teaching students to write place essays when place doesn't really exist?

Marc Augé writes about nonplaces—airports, billboards, and other locations not tied firmly to the ground or existing as unique identities.

As I drive to and from Omaha, an eight-hour drive with wide plains where the mind runs free, I ponder place. I don't know where I can live next, given financial and personal constraints, and I don't know what will feel like home. Little has. I've inhabited so many locations—Toronto, Detroit, Philadelphia, Boston, Amherst, Dallas, Omaha, Boulder—that one wouldn't think moving again would derange me. I love liminality—sunsets, sunrises, spring, fall—why am I so unhinged? If place doesn't exist, if it's only a concoction in my head, what difference does it make? It will be a new place with each passing second.

I should put DFW down.

I can't.

Meanwhile, I-76 is shrouded in greyout, with the high winds, smoke from the fires, and dirt lifted like the Dust Bowl. Towns vanish. In over twenty years, I've never experienced such post-apocalyptic horror. Omaha drifts into nonplace as my mother slows into her nineties. She remains sharp—we watch the VP debate, and although we form political binaries, we agree that we heard content, although none that answered the questions asked.

Maybe I made all these memories up.

DFW concludes by observing that Gödel and Cantor, two of the greatest mathematicians, died in confinement, driven insane lacking that final proof, leaving an unconfined void. "Mathematics continues to get out of bed," he observes wryly. DFW did not continue to touch the floor—he hung himself in 2008, silencing one of the most brilliant essayists in this century.

I'm still lost, in space and time, undecided.

Empty Chairs

LAURIE LEINONEN

There were three springy, white metal chairs practically in the street, behind a house I often passed when heading to a nearby trailhead. I began to notice their arrangement would change, from a traditional three-chair conversational grouping to one chair turned away, separated from the other two, or adjusted to put feet up on one of the others, or lined up in a less conversational row, looking up at the foothills across the street. Sometimes they remained in the same position for days. The arrangement might change slightly . . . due to an animated discussion or a change in the weather, including being frozen in place and untouched when it snowed. Or simply bumped into or pushed out of the way. I always meant to take photographs of their shifting positions but didn't, even while wondering who sat in them and what they might have been discussing. I envisioned happy, engaging conversations, sharing a drink and a snack and an opinion. Or just sitting alone, reading, or thinking or napping. At no time did I ever see a person in any of them. I have no idea when they were used. They were just there. Empty.

As I walk about town, I notice chairs, tables, and hammocks in any number of locations: front or back yards, side gardens, patios, driveways, behind fences, walls, gates, or hedges. Traditional wrought-iron white or black sets. Classic redwood and ubiquitous plastic. There are ones with snowboard seats and backs built with two-by-four frames, as well as the colorful, discarded skis-slatted Adirondack chair. A table made of a slab of slate propped on cement blocks, draped with a brightly patterned oilcloth and a mason jar of dandelions. Chairs shaped out of sections of a downed tree with a stump as a side table. A molded one-piece cardboard chair I assume was likely a design project. Abandoned beer pong tables.

As we enter a pandemic with all its restrictions, I am drawn even more to observe these groupings. I recently passed a beautifully landscaped garden featuring two bright red Adirondack chairs facing out at the street. It was a large, newly built, corner house on a relatively quiet residential street, and, interestingly, they chose to have these two most welcoming, impressive chairs inviting you to sit and literally watch the neighborhood go by. No one was sitting in them. There were a couple of kids on bikes doing tricks around the corner and in the street. I imagined the parents eventually settling into the chairs to admire the young ones' antics as they zipped about.

The pandemic provides a very real possibility to be able to play in the vacant streets as well as for family and friends to watch, oooing and ahhhing, saying hello or nodding to neighbors, dog walkers and passersby. It allows young ones a captive audience while keeping them somewhat in check and provides adults an opportunity for renewed neighborliness. As the lockdown loosens and eventually ends, so will these shared opportunities and experiences. Chances are life will go back to its hectic pace, no matter how inviting an empty chair or two may be.

Dancing Grief

BETH SHAW

Evans, my partner of fifty-plus years, died a couple of weeks ago after a long, debilitating illness. The death was expected and even welcome, but still a shock and a grievous loss for me on some level. I have not experienced many of the obvious, overt symptoms of grief I've observed in some cases—frequent crying spells, loss of sleep and appetite, for example. I've been living on my own for over two years, and the texture of my daily life has changed very little.

The time I do find my grief, or whatever the emotions I'm experiencing after this death might be called, flowing out freely is when I'm dancing. On a few occasions, I've danced with tears streaming down my cheeks (or, more accurately, tears collecting inside my mask). A lyric such as "I'll never let you go" or the poignant song *Midnight Train to Georgia* can elicit this reaction, creating a searing, if momentary, awareness of loss. But I've also felt euphoria—elation—pure joy—as I throw out my arms and open my heart in free and intense movement.

The most important of these moments was a kind of epiphany I experienced where I found myself shouting silently to the world, "We're free! We're free!" This was a moment of great joy and led to a cascade of realizations and a minute but cataclysmic shift in my perspective on my relationship with Evans over the past few years—the period of his illness and decline.

Along with the gradual physical and mental slowing and loss of functionality that were the first symptoms of Evans' Parkinsonism came vague anxieties and fears. He thought "someone" was after his properties and stealing his files. He worried that he was missing meetings that had never been scheduled; that he owed money to "someone" for "something." I tried to be patient with these fears, attempting to reassure him without trying to reason with him (as, reasoning, I read time and time again, doesn't work with someone suffering from dementia). I couldn't always stick to the recommended behavior. I was often impatient with the endless repetition of the same imaginary concerns and then felt guilty for losing patience.

In August of 2019, after a stay in the hospital, Evans moved into an assisted living facility. This was quite a relief for me. I was able to come and go as I pleased, spending time with him when things went smoothly, but free to leave when the paranoia reappeared. I was not so often impatient with him now, but I found new reasons in this new situation to feel guilty. When others visited him, I noticed, he was generally cheerful and made an effort to enter into conversation with them. But when I was alone with him, he often seemed morose and moored in fear and confusion. I often had the sense that I was failing him in some way—not visiting enough, not doing something enough—but what?

After my epiphany on the dance floor, even as I was still dancing, I began to realize that the impetus for this sensation of release and freedom was my sudden understanding that the guilt I had felt all those years had been mostly unwarranted. That what Evans had been looking for from me was not something I could have given him. He was asking me, only me, because he loved and trusted me, to explain, to help, to fix what I had no power to fix. In retrospect, now I suddenly felt honored where I had felt blamed. Now after many long, sad years, we are both free—Evans from the misery, confusion, weakness, and pain of his condition and me, finally and miraculously, from guilt.

The Lunch

MARINA FLORIAN

S ix ladies sat at a glass-topped patio table that had once been my mother's. The table now sat on her best friend's sun-filled porch. It overlooked a vast green lawn with a flagstone terrace and a collection of terracotta pots filled with pink and red geraniums.

The ladies, all close friends of my mother for fifty-odd years, had invited my mother to lunch. The idea was that they wanted to see her as none of them had visited her in her new home, where she had resided for over a year.

My eighty-five-year-old mother had recovered from a debilitating stroke and was now living in a full-care unit at the local nursing home. At the onset of the stroke, at her worst, she had aphasia, i.e., she called a door a "window," was confused, and generally just mixed things up. Now she was considerably more coherent, though not as quick and present as her former self. Yet she was sweeter and kinder.

As the only daughter in a family with three brothers, I had always been at odds with my mother and had resented her dominance over my life. As a typical mother of the 1950s, she saw her role as a disciplinarian, a director of our lives. She felt she was there to make sure that we grew up to be "responsible and valuable members of society." My father was the soft touch who brought a lighter atmosphere and fun when he arrived home from his daily commute to Chicago. I left at sixteen for boarding school and never lived at home permanently again.

As I grew older and took on the main role in caring for my aging parents, I began to know my mother in a new way. We became a team as we looked after my father, who had had many small strokes and was physically challenged.

The day my mother and I arrived for lunch at her old friend's house, the ladies greeted her with enthusiasm. As we began the meal, the conversation quickly drifted off. The women conversed among themselves, citing their favorite topics such as the latest speakers at The Friday Club, a private women's lunch club in Chicago. They spoke of their book club and current events and seemed to forget my mother was there.

I sat beside her and watched her remain pleasant and polite. She was very quiet. I do not know what she was thinking.

I was angry, aghast, hardly believing that these old friends could be so thoughtless. Their superficiality stunned me. Yet, in contrast to these women, I saw my mother in a new light. She was a genuine person and would have never ignored an old friend in such a way.

I still do not know what she felt that day, sitting at the glass-topped patio table that had once been hers. Yet I knew what I felt, and it was deep love and respect for my mother.

A Conversation with the Big Guy

RICHARD MANSBACH

H ey Big Fella

Hello

Wondering if you could answer a few questions in my capacity as the President of my HOA, you know.

Yes. I know.

Oh. Of course, you would. Ahem. My first question is, why are there mosquitoes?

You want to know about mosquitoes during an interview with ME?

Well, I thought it would be a good lead-in, you know, before something more meaty.

Why don't we jump to something meatier now? I do have planets to populate.

Yes. Good point. Um, how about this. Why do you allow horrible, nasty people to live on Earth?

I gave humans free will to explore who they are.

Well, I have some neighbors who are quite unpleasant. They're rude, inconsiderate, and don't follow the rules.

They have forgotten who they are. They have put masks on to play out different roles, and they think that is who they are.

Can't you smite them or something? They're a nuisance.

As I said, free will. By the way, your rules are made from fear.

What do you mean? Without rules, there would be chaos!

You seem to have chaos <u>with</u> the rules. My rule, my religion, is better than yours. That's what your wars are all about.

What are we supposed to do?

Humans come to Earth to learn their unique lesson. Maybe to be the foil for someone else's growth. Maybe for their own growth in overcoming adversity. But the purpose of all of it is to remind them that there is only love.

But what if something wrong was done? In addition to being a nuisance, they don't pay their HOA fees; they park in the wrong place. That really gets my guff. I could go on and on.

Yes, you humans tend to do that.

How am I supposed to love them?

That's the exercise, and the purpose for being on Earth. Humans have created all the discord and forgotten my love for them.

I don't like this exercise!! Can't you send an angel with a magic wand to make everything okay?

I send them all the time. A little kindness here, a little forgiveness there. It seems to take a tragedy for everyone to remember what is important. Love your neighbor as you would love yourself.

Yea. That sounds familiar. I can see I have some work to do.

Anything else?

Oh, one last question. Have you ever interfered with anything on earth?

Well, I did put stickers on all the fruit sold in stores. I thought that was fun.

You did? Why? Peeling those suckers is a pain, and I end up swearing.

Another opportunity to remember love, my dear HOA President.

Thanks, Big Guy.

Dad

LUELLEN RAMEY

The ten-year anniversary of Dad's death is coming up this week. After all these years, I still miss him. I still want to pick up the phone to share good news with him and have more of that one-on-one time with him. There wasn't a dishonest cell in Dad's body, and he never put on airs. It was such a refreshing quality. Dad let me be me, even when my views differed from his, even when he didn't understand the direction I was taking.

William Fletcher Ramey was born in 1925. He was the fifth child in the Ramey family, which made its livelihood on a family farm outside of Rensselaer, Indiana. When he was sixteen, the only child still at home, his father had a stroke, and by necessity, Dad became the family's provider. Because he had to work the farm—both crops and livestock—he missed half of his senior year in high school. Yet he was still the valedictorian of his class.

At twenty-three, he married my mother, Stella List, and she moved in with him and his mother. My sister, Lanny, was born a year later, followed by me a year after that. Lanny and I were together all the time. Dad was successful at farming, and when I was three, we moved to a larger farm a short distance away.

When my sister started school, I didn't realize that I would not also be going. After the first day of school pictures, I followed her to the bus and got on behind her with my dog, Millie. The bus driver then told me that I wasn't old enough for school and Millie and I needed to get off the bus. I hung on to the front gate, crying and watching the bus disappear into the distance. This was a daily occurrence for a couple of weeks.

I hated not being able to go to school, being left behind, and not having anyone to play with during the day. Then Dad said at breakfast, "You're going with me today." Mom had ordered boy clothes for me from the Sears catalog—blue jeans and a denim jacket with a flannel lining and later zip coveralls like my dad wore. I sat on the toolbox on the tractor, holding tight to the fender with both hands, and rode with Dad for hours a day. When he put the truck in first gear to unload hay for the cattle from the back of the truck, I got to steer the truck across the pasture. When he drove around the farm doing errands, I jumped out and opened and closed gates. I handed him tools when he repaired fencing and farm machinery. I helped him nurse sick calves. I felt important, and he trusted me to do things right. I look back now and realize what an atypical solution this was for the time. This was long before "take your daughter to work" days.

Dad worked from sunup to sundown six days a week. On Saturday nights, Mom made popcorn and opened homemade grape juice. I felt safe as I laid in the crook of Dad's arm, and we watched boxing and *Gunsmoke*. The year passed, and it was time to start school, time to leave the boy clothes behind and wear cute dresses with collars and sashes that tied in the back. From the start of school on, gender roles were followed, and I was expected to learn how to cook, bake, sew, garden, and do the things expected of a girl. I spent far less time with Dad.

Dad was smart. He read monthly farming journals and continued to expand his acreage and crops. He was good with carpentry and welding and an astute businessman as well as a farmer. The Indiana governor appointed him to the State Soil and Water Conservation Board. He was well known and well respected in the community and became a mentor to younger farmers in the area. He was a quiet, gentle man, honest, and loyal. Our family attended our Protestant church each Sunday, where Dad was an Elder and on the Board. Although I remember strained times, nagging, and arguments, I'm sure he was faithful to my mother during their sixty-one years of marriage.

Dad had health problems in his mid-sixties—a heart attack and later an aortic aneurism that required a long recovery after surgery. At age sixty-five, he retired from farming and turned the work over to Bob, the younger man who had worked with him for a few decades. Dad spent his time woodworking, maintaining the house, other buildings, and yard, and serving on boards. When Mom died at age eighty-four, Dad was shocked to have outlived her. He had never lived on his own. He was grieving and lonely.

Mom and Dad had two couples that they socialized with each Friday evening and Sundays. By the time Mom died, only Dad and Chris, one of the other women, remained of the six of them. During the two years following Mom's death, I saw Dad's grief slowly replaced by a new love. After sixty-one years of marriage, Dad fell in love with Chris. They never married, but they started each day with a phone call and graced each other's life with love. Dad was affectionate with her, as he had not been with Mom in many years. They demonstrated that you're never too old for new love.

At eighty-six, Dad's health problems were overcoming him, and he was having hospitalizations now and again. I was scheduled to go on a trip to Cambodia and Laos and wondered if I should cancel. I did go, and while there, Dad took a turn for the worse. As soon as I returned to Michigan, I was called to come home. Dad was dying. When I arrived at the hospital, I found out that he had been near death for several days. Bob told me that Dad was hanging on to see me before he died. We put Dad in hospice, and remarkably, he rallied. I was with him each day till he died three weeks later. He was reviewing his life and told me stories. He seemed to have let go of any censoring and relayed to me whatever was on his mind. I learned things about him that I'd never known. The times he was most proud of me. What he thought of this person or that person. What was hardest about his relationship with Mom. It was a poignant and memorable time with Dad.

The way Dad lived exemplified respect with kindness. When age restricted his ability to do manual labor, he found new purpose with his woodworking. Before eldering was a trending topic for aging Baby Boomers, Dad had become a wise elder in his community. He was looked up to for his success and common sense, for his stewardship of the land, and for his caring for his neighbors. He shaped my expectations of what it is to be a whole person.

In Praise of a Variety of Friends

JACK WILLIAMSON

As a clergy person in both civilian and military settings, I've moved more than a dozen times to a new location without knowing anyone. Fortunately, I left each community with a robust group of friends—some having remained over the years, others fading like the morning fog. As I think back, I haven't been very intentional or maybe even conscious about making friends. As an extrovert and a curiosity-driven person, social connections and friendships have evolved naturally.

Maria, one of these friends, grabbed my attention when she suggested that friendships show up in three categories: road friends, silver friends, and gold friends.

"Road friends" are the largest number of friends most of us have. These are wonderful people we meet along the way with whom we mutually resonate. We likely share some facet of life's adventure during a particular chapter of our lives. Characteristically, "road friends" don't imbed themselves in our lives over time. They're great people, but they don't alter our lives.

"Silver friends" are far fewer in number and tend to remain as meaningful friendships as time passes. These people become integral in our lives. In significant ways, they become more important to us than our "road friends." With "silver friends," we navigate tough times together, share momentous events and likely hold similar and deeply held values.

If we are really lucky, we develop one or even a few "gold friends." These are very special people who know and love us as few if any others do—and we them. This is the kind of person who, without hesitation, will gladly sacrifice as much for us as for himself or herself—maybe even more. These rare gems are often closer and dearer than family members, fitting a special category referred to as "family of choice."

Rebecca and I began as strangers living in the same Atlanta, Georgia, neighborhood. During the next fifteen years, we merged into rare "gold friends." Several years ago, in the middle of the night, I received her phone call. Calling from a hospital in Las Vegas, she was in tears and said she needed me to come. Her older brother, Jeff, was in intensive care, dying of AIDS. I took the next flight and was able to be with Rebecca, Jeff, and their elderly mother through his last breaths. Rebecca and I have become deeply connected, laughing, crying, dreaming, and confronting each other. We're "golden."

Michigan State University researcher, William Chopik, indicates that friendships become even more important and powerful as we age. He poignantly adds, "Keeping a few really good friends around can make a world of difference for our health and well-being. It's smart to invest in the friendships that make you happiest."

I'm paying close attention these days to those who enter my life. Now, especially in my elder years, I prize my friends, "road, silver, and gold" because each friend contributes to my well-being and health as I hope I add to theirs.

Bad Boy Dream

LAURA K. DEAL

B y second grade, I already know that Mike is a troublemaker. His blond hair is kept military short, and he hangs out with the other tough kids. He never smiles unless he's laughing at someone. I follow the rules, mostly, and get teased for being book smart. The tough kids frighten me. I already know how people can hurt each other, so I navigate the classroom's social dynamics on high alert. Avoidance is my preference, but sometimes I do daring things to fit in, like ringing the bell on the teacher's desk when she's out of the room, which is strictly forbidden.

Then one night I have a dream that Mike and I kiss. I'm looking into his pale blue eyes, and we ... *like* each other. The day I wake from that dream, I go to school, and all day I sneak glances across the room, trying to understand how I could dream such a dream about *him*. I've never kissed anyone other than my parents. My confusion about Mike lingers for weeks.

Decades later, he sends me a friend request on Facebook. I'm Facebook friends with a lot of my classmates, and since I'm a writer and curious about people, I accept. I soon blocked him from my newsfeed, though. His profile picture is a graphic of a handgun, and he lives in Wyoming, where he repairs guns for a living. His posts are about hunting, the idiots who want gun control, or some violent online game he's playing. I'm still reeling from finding out that a friend's husband threatened her with a gun, not to mention the recurrent trauma of mass shootings in the news. I don't want this extra reminder in my life.

When I post about my daughter's high school switching to a later start time, Mike comments, for the first time ever, on one of my posts, asking which school it is. I hesitate to answer, as all sorts of ugly scenarios play out in my imagination. Has he borne some grudge against me all these years, and now he's going to come to my daughter's school with a gun? A mutual friend reassures me that Mike is safe and it's fine to answer his question. So, I set aside my paranoid fantasies and message him. I don't hear anything more.

A couple of years later, I spend frantic minutes on a bad internet connection refreshing the page, trying to get tickets to see the Dalai Lama. When I'm successful, I announce it on Facebook, too excited not to share. Lots of comments of congratulation pour in, including one from Mike, saying he'd tried once to get tickets to see the Dalai Lama in Salt Lake City, and he would have been happy to drive hours for it, but he wasn't able to get the tickets and had always been disappointed.

Mike? A fan of the Dalai Lama? I stare at the screen, thinking back on my dream from second grade, wondering if I had unconsciously recognized similarities between us that my waking, conscious mind didn't want to see. I can't put it together in my mind that someone who makes his living fixing guns would want to drive hours to hear a holy man who is searching for peaceful solutions to the world's problems.

I never ask him about it.

Mike dies after a sudden illness the day before my fifty-fifth birthday. I hope he found enlightenment. Maybe he'll come and tell me in a dream.

Alexander Marcasite
Marcello Marshmallow

SUSAN JOSEPHS

We went, so I thought, just to look. Gus, our Rottweiler, was aging. Cosmo, our spoiled-to-the-max "Bich-oodle," needed some young blood to boss around.

Sitting on the kitchen floor, we watched Joan's two Standard Poodle puppies interact as this breeder scrutinized us. Being a veterinarian didn't exempt my husband or me from her protective analysis. The little male kept landing in my lap. In between play and cuddling, already showing a hearty appetite for life, he constantly nibbled on kibble. Saturated with the smell of puppy breath and puppy perfume, I got up to leave. With the soft down of puppy promise still lingering, my husband asked, "Which one'll it be?" "Let's think about it," I offered, hoping he'd change his mind. I wasn't looking forward to spending the next several months cleaning up puddles or enduring sleepless nights listening to howls from a crate, feeling the inevitable guilt, while our other dogs slept on our bed. But my husband wasn't to be sidetracked. "Which one?" he reiterated.

I'd already fallen in love. "Let's take the male."

Paperwork completed, we headed home in Michael's two-month-old BMW with our pup on a towel in my lap. As we got on the highway, I was ungraciously reminded of his enormous appetite. I had heard muffled warning sounds moments before he started throwing up. I opened the window, offering fresh air. I massaged his belly. Nothing relieved him. My husband drove faster, attempting to shorten the time the product of puppy fear and gorging bombarded his brand-new car.

The siren and whirling lights appeared in our rearview mirror. Michael pulled over; our little fluffball was still heaving. "Hello, officer. I know I was going too fast. I'm a veterinarian trying to get this sick dog back to my practice;" he stretched the truth a bit.

The officer looked in the car and saw the soiled towels and the piles of soppy paper. He was not the animal lover we needed him to be.

How could anyone look into those pitiful eyes and still say, "License and registration?" We'd add $135 to the price of this puppy.

Alexander Marcasite Marcello Marshmallow. It was a big name to give to a tiny puppy, but we suspected he'd grow into it. "Marcello" because his eyes were reminiscent of the Italian heartthrob, Marcello Mastroianni. Our daughter added, "Marshmallow"; it represented his inner mush.

He'd sprawl out on our bed, where nothing could budge him. Entertaining onlookers, he'd do somersaults in mid-air to retrieve a flying squirrel toy. A Houdini escape artist, Marcello would climb over the top of one of our veterinary hospital's chain-link kennel doors to get closer to Michael. On off-leash walks, he acted like the mayor, attaching himself to people, not other dogs. Marcello graced us for thirteen and a half years. Bred for companionship, even when critically ill, he'd move from one spot to another to be near us.

We have owned eleven dogs altogether. My husband still sobs when looking at videos of our beloved companion. Marcello's Memory Garden blooms in our backyard, reminding us of his devotion to us and ours to him. Marcello, you were our heart-dog. The emptiness lingers forever.

Appalachian Birth

JANAT HOROWITZ

"Take off everything but your socks," she said. *I must have heard that wrong*, I thought. So I sat there, in a dingy doctor's office on a cracked brown leather chair and waited for the weathered nurse to return. Which she did and growled, "You're still dressed; take everything off but your socks and lay on the table." I was nineteen years old at the time, on a college campus in rural West Virginia. There was only one OB/GYN in a forty-mile radius, and he primarily raised cattle. I stripped to my socks, got up on the table, and placed my feet in the stirrups. Oh boy, this was all new to me, and the doctor, whose hands were five times the size of mine, said, "You're pregnant." Those two words changed my life and body forever.

Ten months later, not nine, I had gained enough weight to birth a two-year-old heifer. My life had changed so dramatically, I couldn't believe it. I ate constantly to comfort myself. I had always been thin with long, skinny legs, but now my belly was gargantuan, and I had no idea of the dangers of gaining so much weight. I was really a child—a child who had happened to have had sex.

Unbelievably, I started having regular contractions right there, but as soon as the doctor came in to check me with his sumo-sized hands, they stopped immediately. After eleven days in the hospital, though I enjoyed receiving meals and back rubs nightly, I wanted to go home and sleep in my own bed.

My first night home, my labor resumed right away, and as I had been trained the previous eleven days, I waited until they were five minutes apart. Then I went back to the hospital, where I shared a room with two other women from town, also in labor. They told me that between them, they had thirty-one children. "Honey, I'd have seventeen more if my body'd hold up." (Them's was Philippi, West Virginia, folks!) At some point, the cattle doctor reached inside me and said, "I cain't budge her; we're going to have to do a C-section." Hallelujah, this hell was going to end soon!

Little did I know that it would take me decades to heal from this. That cowboy doctor left me with a scar from my pubic bone to my navel that wasn't sewn up right and had a couple twists and turns. My sweet, young body was now scarred and stretched in a way I had no idea was possible. For decades, I blamed myself for everything that had happened to me there.

Years later, working and living at the clothing-optional Esalen Institute in Big Sur, California, I was naked in the hot mineral baths with thousands of other naked bodies. Being there among women with scars like mine from mastectomies and the like finally healed my body shame. I learned that bodies reveal a person's history, and I grew to love and admire this body that has always done what I've asked it to do: climb mountains, ski, pilot rafts down rivers, birth another baby girl (not traumatic at all), and snuggle with my beloved, who loves my body, too!

The In-Between

SARAH MASSEY-WARREN

We're going to teach them how to say good-bye, say good-bye, one last time.

—Lin-Manuel Miranda

Hay bales curl into the ground like porcupines. Wolf trees fan their canopies. Corn stalks, relieved of tasseled ears, guard the fields. Birds dip into retention ponds mid-route between hither and yon. Hills morph into buttes. I'm anywhere in between North Platte and Jarlsberg, my windows closed, my iPhone playing music ranging from 1600 to now, rock to classical, Railroad Earth to Bach. I dodge Labor Day cars and semis and look back in the mirror at the large *Clivia*, whose frond-like leaves devour the entirety of my hatchback.

Days earlier, I sit with my mom in her assisted living apartment, a place that she swore she would go to "over her dead body." She has roller-coastered here after a swift series of visits to hospitals and skilled nursing care over the course of a month. We watch films for hours: *Joy Luck Club, Dances with Wolves, My Fair Lady, Rain Man, Big Night, Breakfast at Tiffany's.* In the courtyard, we suck in every detail of the flowers and fountain. Mentally sharp, she smiles wryly and asks, "Have you even noticed what day it is?" Hospice visits several times a week for issues related to congestive heart failure. Freed from toxic medicines, she's finally eating again. We consume catfish dinners from Surfside Club, a cult destination next to the Missouri River, marinated lemon cucumbers from my garden, and spring rolls and wontons from Panda Express. The size of RBG, my mom suffers from swollen legs that began to "weep" while I visit, plummeting our moods. Like RBG, she worked until she turned ninety-one. We bury our heads in Netflix like ostriches. We skirt feelings.

I stay at her house in north Omaha. Nestled into an oak ravine, it won a *Progressive Architecture* Award—a modern drainage solution to building on a steep slope in heavy trees. An open space plan, the rooms swim into each other on two floors. The living room windows stretch for two stories. I spend late nights there watching thunderstorms, the lightning painting the panes of glass in jagged streaks. Outside on the deck, blue jays, wrens, hummingbirds, woodpeckers, cardinals, and tangiers perch on the two birdfeeders, making the living room a better yoga space than any found in Boulder. My mother's paintings and other artwork and artifacts gathered from around the world, as well as family photos, line the cedar walls. Flowering annuals fill the deck. Strangers knock at the door, asking to tour. No wonder she didn't want to leave. The house is a soulless shell without her.

In *Lincoln in the Bardo*, George Saunders describes Abraham Lincoln's visits to his dead son's body in the vault where he is buried, as the ghosts of the newly dead linger and watch. He writes, "Only then (nearly out the door, so to speak) did I realize how unspeakably beautiful all of this was, how precisely engineered for our pleasure, and saw that I was on the brink of squandering a wondrous gift, the gift of being allowed, every day, to wander this vast sensual paradise, this grand marketplace lovingly stocked with every sublime thing."

As I drive, I recall the distinct aesthetic my mother has created in her work, the singular gift store, and home—her legacy. I notice every bush, every bird I pass. Near Big Springs, the stench of a slaughterhouse seeps into my nose. A few miles later, cows and calves savor every blade of grass. I-80 swells with unspeakable gifts, each one echoing Mary Oliver's demand to her reader: "Tell me, what is it you plan to do with your one wild and precious life?"

Parhelia

PEGGY WALLIS

I 've heard that somewhere in the northern part of Scotland, when the temperature is very low, there can appear to be three suns in the sky. Phantom suns, Parhelia, are sometimes called sun dogs. The middle sun is the brightest, with the other two appearing to be slightly smaller and hazier. These satellite suns, flanking the middle, fiery sphere, come from reflected light. It has something to do with ice crystals. Sinking through the air, these crystals become vertically aligned, refracting the sunlight horizontally so that there appear to be suns in triplicate. Sometimes, this refracted sunlight will create a halo around the sun as well. It is said that three suns in the sky herald the start of a great storm, perhaps an Ice Age. If so, the present Ice Age, predicted in the heavens, is a cold age of meanness and vanity; a great storm of cruelty to others.

I've also heard this. It has been told that the sun was so enamored of her beauty that she created the moon as a mirror to endlessly reflect her image. Moonlight, sunlight, and darkness—there are so many types of reflections that it can be hard to produce a stable self-image. Such is the transformative nature of light and dark, the wide range of colors produced by its spectrum. Often, I am blinded by that light. I am the middle sun, reflecting light to create hazy images of myself. What about my children? Are they my sun dogs, my antidote to the fading light, to the inevitable darkness? But, at other times, that reflected light is gone, absorbed by the darkness, eclipsed by my own mirrored moon, and erased by the great storm of anger that overtakes me.

My children are grown now, shining with their own light. They glow as if they had nursed upon my sunlight, gained energy from it, and reflected that light back onto the world as it became their own. Each has, with the passage of time, become their own middle sun. And, in doing so, they have created their own smaller images, phantom suns, Parhelia. As the days grow colder and colder, with the world becoming meaner, they warm my present and light the future.

So to my reflected suns, my lovely Parhelia, I would say, "Shine brightly. The world needs your energy. It is better to be kind than smart. Don't mistake your reflection, your empty image, your moon mirror, for the real thing."

The Journey—
Upward and Inward

MARY ANN PALIANI

Have you ever daydreamed about doing something out of the ordinary, then quickly discarded the idea because you believed that you lacked the ability? Have you ever wondered, *What are my limits—physical, intellectual, emotional?*

A year ago, while climbing the Flattop Mountain trail in Rocky Mountain National Park, my guide, Bob, and I reached a lookout on the trail that gave us an unobstructed view of Long's Peak, and it's very daunting North Face. As we looked out over the landscape, Bob asked me if I might ever consider climbing Long's by the technical North Face route. My immediate reaction was, "Out of the question. I can't do that." Fast forward to August 27, 2019. Around 12:30 p.m. on that day, I found myself on the Long's summit, at the ripe old age of eighty-four, after reaching it via the technical North Face.

What was the odyssey between "I can't do it" and "I did it?" And what did I learn? The North Face is a technical route with fifth class terrain. The entire expedition, from the Boulder Fields (12,760 feet) to the summit (14,259 feet) and back again, took sixteen hours, four of which were spent climbing in the dark, and involved navigating over a complex, steep, and very treacherous terrain without trails. Though I had trained for Long's for many months, I had not, as yet, undergone the experience of handling significant and prolonged exertions at altitudes over 14,000 feet. There was the additional challenge of maintaining continuous and intense focus on every step that I took. One misstep, on a loose rock, or a stumble could have serious consequences. The mental effort was almost greater than the physical demands. Finally, I had to reckon with the descent. A view of the descent from the summit underscored the challenge ahead. The climb down, into an ever-darkening abyss as night came upon us, promised to be exciting. At this point, despite an ever-growing, gut-wrenching anxiety, my options were limited to one: go forward and downward, one step at a time! For the last two hours of the descent, I had to depend on the light from my headlamp to navigate over and around giant boulders. The entire experience was the ultimate test of one's physical, mental, and emotional endurance.

Further, the intense focus the climb demanded taught me what it meant to live in the moment. I came to regard each second of my life on that mountain as an exotic jewel with facets of joy, fear, accomplishment, and pain. Taken together, I realized that they contributed to the fabric of my life—a work of art—and were priceless!

Ultimately, Long's was much more than a wilderness adventure. It was a critical emotional and spiritual journey that allowed me to catch a glimpse of who I am and what I can do as I pursue a lifelong search for my identity.

The Best Dance Ever

RICHARD MANSBACH

H ospice. A recurrence of cancer. Metastasized nine years later to the brain. My adult daughter and I were caring for my wife, Susan, in our home.

Discovered the cancer after she fell from a bike, when she broke an orbital bone. After the MRI, the nurse looked me in the eye and said, twice, in a serious voice, "You need to see a doctor," without telling me what was on the X-ray.

The hospital back home called us to set up an appointment. There, we walked into a room with a doctor and four others in lab coats. I guessed later that they were there in case we broke down. Two for each of us. He handed an X-ray of my wife's brain to us, and it was mostly white. That was the cancer. All my wife and I could say was, "Wow." We both saw it from a place of curiosity and spirituality. How did this happen?

Susan cared deeply about the injustices in the world. Before the fall, she had talked about walking across America as a peace pilgrim. She had been on staff for the Hunger Project and had an affinity for mothers and newborns as a doula. Near the end, having lost sight in one eye, I remember her sitting cross-legged on the couch, and with heart-breaking sobs, asking why children died in this world. It is my belief that she couldn't stand it anymore and wanted to leave the planet to assist from the spiritual world.

Radiation was started while Susan continued with life, taking long walks and journaling. Given six months, she lived for seven. The last two weeks, she was bedridden.

My daughter and I both had been trained in basic nursing and bedside skills. I controlled the IV drip and didn't want Susan to suffer. My daughter preferred a smaller dosage to support my wife in being more conscious.

I would swing and lift Susan into a sitting position on the edge of the bed, then, grabbing under the arms, stand her up and hold her while my daughter cleaned and changed the diaper. I said, "What a wonderful dance," and she would say, "The best dance ever."

A couple of days before she passed, she sat bolt straight up and expressed, in a strong voice, her displeasure with me over old scars. The rest of hospice time, we expressed our deep love for each other, cried and laughed together, and reminisced. We were complete, having said it all.

Friends came over to say goodbye. The day Susan passed away, I had just taken a shower when I was urgently called into her room. I missed her last breath by a minute. I guess she wanted it that way.

That night, I had just gotten into bed when I saw a bright, silver-dollar-size starlight streak from left to right at the foot of the bed. I was amazed, and then I smiled, acknowledging the thin curtain between here and there.

Trading a Ford for a BMW

MARINA FLORIAN

I t was a typical, blistering hot August in Walnut Creek, California. My ten-year-old stepdaughter was visiting from Michigan for a month, and I was commuting daily to San Francisco on BART, working as a project manager in the Facilities Department at the Bank of California.

Having Valerie, a bouncy, energetic presence in our house, was always a treat. My husband, Jerry, was helpful but left the bulk of the work to me. I took the lead in organizing her summer—swimming in the outdoor neighborhood pool, shopping and eating hot dogs at Target, and walking with our two feisty golden retrievers. Jerry even left us one weekend to go to Lake Tahoe with a friend.

On evening walks with our dogs in our suburban neighborhood, Jerry and I caught up with each other. One night, just after Valerie had left, he repeated a refrain that I had heard all summer. "Well, *you* don't like to go bicycling" and *"You* don't like Lake Tahoe." I offered that I would be happy to try bicycling; I just hadn't had the time. As for Lake Tahoe, he was right—I did not like the area that he preferred, which involved drinking and gambling.

Then, as we strolled, I had an epiphany. "Is there someone else who likes these things?" I asked him, and he simply replied, "Yes." From that moment on, my settled, married world was shattered.

I continued working and relied on my many friends to comfort me, but my core sense of stability was blown apart. The thought of being on my own, at age forty-four, without a house and a stable partner was frightening to me.

Yet, as Thanksgiving rolled around, I accepted an invitation to stay with my best friend at her parents' house in Vail, Colorado. On Thanksgiving Day, we skied and then rushed around making a Jack Daniel's sweet potato dish for a dinner party. As we drove to her friends' house, she suggested I take off my wedding ring. I was surprised at this idea but conceded.

The dinner party was made up of about ten guests, some married, some not. I was seated next to Harry, a guy from Rifle, Colorado; we discussed our Philadelphia connections and discovered we were exactly the same age. Later, in the kitchen, we both helped Anne, our hostess, wash the multiple dirty dishes.

To my surprise, the next day, Harry called. We had dinner that evening in Minturn at "The Saloon," a local Mexican restaurant, and our affair began.

Harry worked at Colorado Mountain College in Rifle, Colorado as the campus dean, participating in everything from signing checks to helping at the front desk. To all concerned, he was a wonderful person, and I soon felt the same way.

A year later, at another Thanksgiving dinner, now at my house in California, a close friend and work colleague summed up my recent experience. Helping himself to another serving of turkey, he casually remarked, "Well, I believe you have traded in a Ford for a BMW."

On Being Alone in the Dark for These Dark Times

JACK WILLIAMSON

'm an early-to-bed, early-to-rise guy. I used to fight this pattern and periodically felt degrees of shame in admitting it to others. I have since accepted that neither early down nor early up are clear choices, but rather attributable to my natural, nocturnal rhythms.

I often find that waking up and getting out of bed in the early-morning darkness offers particular opportunities that can dissipate like the morning dew when the light of day arrives. On these occasions, I go to my office and sit alone in my very comfy recliner while being ushered into zones of introspection, creative thoughts, and inspiration. I find this qualitative quiet time facilitates a gentle personal presence and a preparation for the opportunities and challenges a new day will present. Sometimes I write in the dark, like essay drafts; occasionally, I record my voice; mostly, I listen to the "sounds of silence." These valued moments of solitude offer a gift of focus, allowing space to tune into my quiet inner center.

I find Shirley Murray's eloquent lyrics a helpful prompt from time to time:

Come and find the quiet center in the crowded life we lead,
find the room for hope to enter, find the frame where we
are freed:
clear the chaos and the clutter, clear our eyes, that we
can see all the things that really matter, be at peace, and
simply be.
Silence is a friend who claims us, cools the heat and slows
the pace,
making space within our thinking, lifting shade to show
the light.

Renowned Buddhist writer, Stephen Batchelor, in his book, *Alone with Others*, speaks of the paradox of "always finding ourselves inescapably *alone* and at the same time inescapably *together with others*." He calls this understanding of human fulfillment *awakening*, as the integration of wisdom *(alone)* and compassion *(with others)*.

But there is another kind of darkness—the dark times we are all currently living in. It is an absence of light, of understanding, that few if any of us could have imagined just a few months ago. So many parts of our lives are clouded with uncertainty and fear—disrupted and changed with no timeline of returning to former or even new normals.

During these dark days, my night-dreams seem to be increasing and are becoming more vivid and weird. The Lyon Neuroscience Research Center helps explain why. Essentially, when our fears are hard to face or visualize, our brain creates metaphors—often vivid. The transition from my sleeping mind to my awaking mind seeks to make sense of these metaphoric dreams. It also offers a bridge for integrating my wisdom *(alone)* and compassion *(with others)*.

Our prolonged pandemic situational and societal darkness reminds me to seek and cherish my early morning moments of solitude now more than ever.

During the darkness of sky or of life, I am grateful for the gift and importance of solitude that breathes light and aliveness into my life. David Whyte, the Irish poet, nails it for me when he says:

> Sometimes it takes darkness and the sweet
> confinement of your aloneness
> to learn
> anything or anyone
> that does not bring you alive
> is too small for you.

A Funny Thing Happened on the Way

JEFFREY PEACOCK

I have been traveling around the world in airplanes for sixty-five years. From north to south and east to west. Many unusual events have taken place during my journeys, but the weirdest things always seemed to occur during my travels in the Arab world.

Goats and parrots in the cabin, oh yes! First class seats reserved by wealthy Saudis for their new Michelin tires, yes again. During a flight out of Sanaa, Yemen, in 1973, I was handed a one-year-old baby with a very full diaper to be held during take-off. A Yemeni mother had boarded with eight children and one ticket. Each of us in the first-class cabin was asked to hold one of her children as the plane took off. The baby who I was asked to take care of was screaming, and I was praying that his nappy would not spill over before I could return him to his mother.

My next adventure occurred on a flight from Beirut, Lebanon, to Jeddah, Saudi Arabia. Shortly after takeoff, the pilot announced, "We must return to Beirut because the plane is losing hydraulic fuel." From my window seat, I could see a gusher of liquid streaming back from the wing. We successfully landed, but due to the loss of hydraulic fluid, we had no brakes, just the engine reversers to slow us down. We finally rolled to a stop with the plane's nose hanging over the end of the runway and a sheer drop to the sea.

After a six-hour wait in a deserted airport, we boarded another aircraft. Unfortunately, it was a smaller airplane with twenty fewer seats. Luckily, I boarded near the front of the queue and quickly seated myself. Those behind me were less fortunate, and fist-fights broke out, requiring ambulances for those injured in the battle for seats. After we took off, the pilot announced that we were flying to Riyadh, Saudi Arabia, instead of to Jeddah, which was our original destination.

Several months later, I was seated on a flight between Riyadh—the Saudi capital—and Jeddah, where the American embassy was located in those days, when a desert Bedouin was seated next to me. He had never traveled on an airplane and happily knelt on the seat with folded legs. Despite repeated admonishments from the flight attendant, he refused to seat himself properly.

After leveling off, we were served hot tea by the cabin crew. My companion from the desert had no idea how to hold a cup with a handle. He did not realize that he needed to exert pressure on the handle to prevent spillage as the cup filled. As a result, the hot tea from his cup spilled onto my lap.

Later in the flight, my Saudi "friend" had to relieve his bladder. He went forward where he entered one of the two toilets available. Taking advantage of his absence, I, too, went to the lavatory. Seeing the "non-occupied" sign on one door, I opened the door only to discover my seatmate squatting with his feet on the toilet seat. He was holding his thobe (an ankle-length garment) up with his right hand and himself with his left hand. Startled by the opening of the door, he decided to remove his left hand from his "manhood" in an attempt to swing the door shut. This caused his appendage to elevate due to a very full stream of urine. The urine hosed across my trouser legs before the door was closed. A female flight attendant dried me off and moved me up to the first-class cabin.

My flight was fully reimbursed, and a letter of abject apology was mailed to the American embassy by the airline. Indeed, "a funny thing happened on the way!"

Buddy

BETH SHAW

I 'm a cat person. There has been a cat in my life most of the time for as long as I can remember: Chi Chi when I was very young, then Puff, a pure white male who started as a ball of fluff but grew into a strong, macho predator who nevertheless melted under my caresses and fed my fantasies of animal-as-prince. Over the years, there have been a series of others: Tiger, Pia, Paka, Snow, Missy, Spots, and last but hardly the least, Sophie, my precious little fifteen-year-old perpetual kitten.

In Philip Pullman's young adult fantasy, *The Golden Compass*, every character has a *daemon*, a spiritual companion, that takes the form of an animal and is connected to the human soul by an invisible thread. If that thread is broken, the human may not die, but his/her spirit is destroyed. When I first encountered that concept (as a fairly old adult, actually), it struck a chord with me. It seemed to express perfectly the deep, almost magical connection one has with a truly beloved pet.

I like dogs but had never wanted one. When my stepsons moved in with my husband, Evans, and me, they had King, a handsome shepherd/husky mix, who lived with us for several years. I liked him, but Paka, my cat at the time, was my true soulmate. Then, about thirteen years ago, my husband decided he wanted a beagle. I was not enthusiastic about the idea. His grand-daughter had a beagle puppy—cute, to be sure, but he howled and chewed things up and terrorized two-year-old Sophie. Nevertheless. Evans eventually found Buddy, an eighteen-month-old beagle, at a humane society shelter and brought him home one January while I was away for a few days.

At first, our relations were civil but fairly cool. Sophie and I were able to convince Buddy quite quickly that she was the alpha pet. I've come to regret the absolute nature of that lesson, as she has taken advantage of it over the years, and sweet Buddy still cowers at the foot of stairs and outside doorways if she decides to stand in his way. I've grown extremely fond of him, and have learned how truly intuitive, sensitive, funny, and communicative dogs can be. Don't get me wrong. Sophie is still my little soul sister, and if I ever have another pet, I'm sure it will be a cat, but Buddy has been a joy and becomes a closer friend every year.

For many years, Buddy and Evans were inseparable. Evans walked him twice a day, fed him, took him everywhere with him in his truck, but as age and dementia started taking a toll, I gradually took over. A couple of years ago, Buddy developed melanoma in his mouth, and on the advice of a friend who is a retired vet, we subjected him to a painful series of melanoma vaccine injections and jaw surgery. To my great joy, this regimen seems to have worked, as Buddy is still going strong at fourteen-plus years old. Although he now seeks care and attention, Buddy still spends much of his time by Evans' side. Evans is still who he cares about most deeply, and that's fine with me. I'm so grateful he's still here to support me in this difficult time. He's not my *daemon*. I'll always be a cat person, but there will always be a huge and very special place in my heart for the best Buddy ever.

Black or White?

LUELLEN RAMEY

The Black Lives Matter movement has caused me to recall the only time in my life that I was ever mistaken for a Black person. It was 1974, and Reggie and his friends lived in an impoverished Black neighborhood in Pompano Beach, Florida. This city had a harness racetrack. There was running water for the horses at the racetrack but not for the poor Blacks, who lived in small shacks across the street. Most of Pompano Beach was middle-class or upscale, closer to the ocean. But these folks made their living picking peas and beans that grew in the land adjacent to the Everglades. These Black families stayed in their ghetto, while most Whites made drastic detours through Pompano Beach to totally avoid this area. Although only eight miles inland from the Atlantic coast, many of these children had never seen the ocean.

I was a speech and language clinician working for the Broward County schools. One of my assigned schools was Markham Elementary in this Black neighborhood. Due to its special status from the Department of Health, Education, and Welfare (HEW), Markham Elementary remained a segregated school that had a lot of government funds channeled into it. Students got both breakfast and lunch at the school; sometimes, their only food. Most of their health care was provided by the school nurse. Parents worked long hours and rarely showed up at the school.

One of my favorite groups to work with in this school was a small group of first-grade boys. In addition to articulation, I taught them Standard American English, which we called White Talk. In turn, they got to teach me Black dialect. It was a fun exchange, and they would roar with laughter at my Black Talk and correct me till I got it right.

I let them tell me what would motivate them. They wanted to push a broom beside Mr. Johnson, the janitor who had great cachet with the kids. Mr. Johnson was game, so that and fresh mangoes became their chosen rewards for good work in this group.

One day, I came into the room, and the boys were having a lively discussion about whether I was Black or White. Reggie, one of the most vocal, kept insisting that I was Black. James jumped on my lap, put his arm next to mine, and proclaimed, "She be a White lady!" They wanted to know the answer to their question, and I said, "I'm White." Reggie got this pouty look on his face, and I asked him why he thought I was Black. His answer was, "Because you're nice, and I like you." I have always remembered the implications of that answer.

A Transformative Experience

MARY ANN PALIANI

The scene in front of me was at once majestic and terrifying! The night before, a heavy snowfall had blanketed this lonely and isolated spot in the Swiss Alps. The towering Eiger, Mönch and Jungfrau stood like fearsome sentinels over a world shrouded in mist and entombed in ice and snow. Drifts reached the eaves of the isolated Kleine Scheidegg hotel, where I was staying. The wraithlike figures on the ski lift appeared like a procession of recently departed souls disappearing into a grey, otherworldly dimension. The snow and limited visibility made it impossible to judge ski conditions and terrain.

Contributing to a feeling of dread and foreboding was the hotel itself. Built years ago, it was an old structure with an ambience reminiscent of a bygone age. It had the haunting quality of the Outlook Hotel in *The Shining*. One of its more macabre offerings was the ability to view, through a telescope in its parlor, the corpse of a climber still hanging from the deadly Eiger.

On this first morning of my five-day ski vacation, I was convinced that my limited skiing experience in Vermont in no way prepared me for the challenge ahead. I was in way over my head—and terrified!

However, I hated to just give up. So I went to a ski patrolman for guidance. He brusquely asked if I could snowplow. I said, "Yes." He replied, "Go," and pointed to a T-bar, the only lift that served the area. So, with great trepidation, I got in line. The person with whom I shared the lift was a huge man, who was probably twice my weight and at least a foot taller. On a T-bar, this is not an ideal arrangement. As the lighter person, I would have to exert considerable force to counterbalance my heavier companion.

By the time I got on the lift, I was in a state of panic and trembling uncontrollably. Perceiving my state of mind (or more accurately, feeling it from the shaking lift), my partner cavalierly advised me that should I fall off, to just hang onto the lift's horizontal bar. He would then counterbalance the T-bar and drag me to the top. But seconds later, instead of *my* falling off, **he did**—and he hung on! In a heartbeat, I was the one offsetting over 200 pounds of drag. Instinctively, I braced my body like a steel rod against the ski track, while exerting Herculean strength to maintain the stance. My mind emptied, but for one thought—brace! Fear disappeared.

We reached the top. It was time to exit the lift. Without any warning, my companion let go. Caught off guard, I found myself still gripping the lift as it suddenly started spinning like a top. I was trapped in a vortex that kept me pinned to it. Meanwhile, the T-bar was now moving, at what seemed like blinding speed, toward a huge barricade, against which it would slam (and me with it) before returning to the base. I had just nanoseconds to act before the impact. As I spun around, I caught fleeting glimpses of the lift line below me, the barricade straight ahead, and the mountainous snow pile to my right. My only escape route was the ski track on my left. But could I, at just the right moment and place, overcome this impossible force that kept me in its embrace? Then, out of nowhere, that mysterious strength within me once again asserted itself. And suddenly, I was free—and safe!

I had survived! And with that realization came an epiphany: I had just experienced a life-changing discovery. Some mysterious power within me had suddenly and automatically transformed paralyzing fear into awesome strength.

Dominion

LAURA K. DEAL

In Genesis 1:26, we're told that God gave humans dominion over fish, fowl, cattle, and everything that creeps on the earth. We humans like to believe it. God gave us clever brains, nimble fingers, and stories. We put them all to use, shaping our environment to suit our essential needs, and to fulfill our selfless or greedy desires. We don't always find the best paths, nor even agree on whether the needs of all matter more than the desires of the few. We cooperate and compete. We're complex animals, living in a matrix of life on this planet that consists of networks we can't even imagine. Yet we can trace our connections to those networks through the air we breathe and the water we drink, if nothing else.

We like to believe we have dominion, and perhaps that's why some of us strip ecosystems bare for one asset or another. Maybe that's why pyromaniacs light fires. Maybe that's at the heart of my urge to garden, though I hope I work in concert with nature, taking into account how to enrich the soil with compost and how to reduce water needs, learning what plants grow well together, and saving seeds.

Genesis tells us God gave us dominion, but elsewhere in the Bible, we're warned of the whirlwind, of God's wrath visited upon the wicked by storm and whirlwind. (Nahum 1:3-1:6) We were given dominion, but paradoxically, nature always has her way. When I was a child, I couldn't understand why someone hadn't figured out how to keep the weather away. I wasn't thinking personal raingear, but some giant shield over everything. I didn't understand, nor even wonder about, the air that filled my lungs; how it rushed in from near and far, bearing ash from distant volcanic eruptions, or smoke from far off fires. I thought as I'd been taught. We humans were in charge of the land and animals. So why not the weather?

As I got older, and my family experienced floods, hailstorms, and the smoke from wildfires, I understood on a fundamental level that when it wants, the weather controls us. It's no wonder that people dream of tornadoes when the world feels alarming. People share new dreams almost every week on my blog post about tornadoes as a dream symbol. Tornadoes speak to us of the great uncertainties of our times. How can a virus sweep through a population and leave one person asymptomatic and the next dead? How can tornadoes leave one house untouched and reduce the one beside it to rubble?

We can choose to see the COVID-19 pandemic as God's wrath, as a chastening time. With our magnificent brains, we found paths forward to lessen the impact of the virus. Perhaps we can also find ways to lessen the severe weather that will come with climate change. We might discover that flying across the country for a meeting isn't necessary. Some might give up commuting altogether. However, some of us will cling to a belief in our dominion and swagger into public spaces unmasked and fail to curtail our consumeristic lifestyles. Others of us will see our dominion residing in scientific understanding, and we'll try to stop the pandemic's spread as effectively as possible, taking every precaution. With any luck, we'll turn our attention next to solving and surviving climate change.

Awakening to Self-Care

JANAT HOROWITZ

It started with getting ripped off by an online concert ticket scammer. This guy was good! He talked in a soft way and had little children's voices playing in the background. I was 95 percent sure I could trust him. The minute I said, "The money is in your account," he hung up. When I called back, the message was, "This phone has been disconnected."

The anger and shame that filled me gave me a tight feeling in my chest. As I had tachycardia last year, alarms went off as my heartbeat started to race. I started measuring my blood pressure, and it was all over the place. When I told my doctor, she put me on blood pressure medicine. That experience led to my husband and me becoming fearful that I could have a stroke or heart attack. He said if I died of either, he would kill me. Shortly after getting off the medication, my blood pressure stabilized.

What came out of the above was realizing that stress was one of my challenges. *How can I take better care of me?* I wondered, and began to take a personal inventory. On the enneagram, a Sufi system of psychological typing, I'm a "9." We are the type that loves comfort and ease and we avoid conflict. With that aim, we often merge with others to the point of forgetting ourselves. We will distract ourselves and look the other way to keep the peace. Working for a perfectionist, controlling woman these past few years, who neurotically micromanages me, has been stressful. Having grandchildren, I know by now how to make a scrambled egg, but she stands over me to make sure I do it "her way." She is an addict in recovery, and I have supported her in staying off opioids. How do you care for yourself when working for a boss like this?

After being her assistant for five years, this week I gave my two-week notice. There have been thoughts of quitting for a couple of months, but the other day, when she had a stomachache and started slurring her words, a feeling of dread arose in me, and I'd had enough. Years ago, when she got clean—and what a nightmare for me she was in that detoxification process—I told her I wouldn't go through this again. When I gave my notice, it was not easy, but she could understand when I said I need to take care of myself, and I immediately felt a giant surge of relief.

Having taken care of myself in this situation, I now look forward to learning more about self-care. Self-care is not something most of us Boomer women learned. We were brought up to be "sugar and spice and everything nice" and to please everyone. It's great to see our daughters and granddaughters learning something else.

Wrinkles and Time

SUSAN JOSEPHS

I have a complicated relationship with ironing. I've decorated my mother Esther's ironing board, layering its wooden surface with her antimacassars, Italian linen hand towels, and embroidered lace runners. It is my shrine to her. Perched on its narrow surface are family photographs, Mom's clothespins held in the silk, a hand-crocheted bag that her mother, my Grandmother Sadie, made. This same surface was once home to laundered underwear, towels, sheets, shirts, and dresses that were sprinkled with water and starched and ironed. But I don't iron.

In her farewell tribute to the outrageous, grander-than-life, fashionista, André Leon Talley, Maureen Dowd reminds me of my ambiguous relationship to ironing. André was friends with Tom Ford, Andy Warhol, Vogue's Anna Wintour, and most of the who's who in society and fashion. He dressed Michelle Obama and Jackie O. Just out of college, André became Diana Vreeland's unpaid intern, helping curate the Metropolitan Museum of Art's fashion exhibits. His grandmother ironed André's boxer shorts and towels. He understood why Vreeland ironed her dollar bills and tissues. Crispness was everything.

I, too, understand the allure of crispness. I appreciate the feel of a smooth garment. But I don't iron. "Is that a surfboard, Mom?" my kids asked when they saw my dusty, obligatory ironing board hanging on the laundry room door. My conflict—loving all things crisp but refusing to unwrinkle even my most ashamedly creased collection of linen shirts—may have been solved with an unexpected discovery.

In 2015, an Ancestry email alerted me to an unknown relation. The sender was a friend of my potential relative. Deb had just learned we were halfsisters. I was shocked to discover that Deb was just five years younger than me. Deb's friend told me that Deb's mother, Helen, used to work for us. I have such vivid memories of Deb's mother coming to our Manhattan apartment and laboring over the piles of wrinkled garments which she magically transformed into folded or hung, pressed, crisp masterpieces.

But I couldn't rectify the image of sweet Helen with another distant memory of an angry, unhappy woman, whom I *also* remember. Then Deb reminded me that her Aunt Maude, who worked for another family in our building, had introduced Helen to my mother. Mom hired Maude's young sister. Once I discovered my new sister Deb, I realized that Maude would have known that my father was her niece's dad. I had always felt guilty, thinking Maude begrudged having to work for a white family. But I finally understood Maude's anger; she must have been furious with my father for impregnating her sister. My memory of Maude had been confused with my memory of Helen.

My sister Deb and I text, speak, and look forward to meeting when this crazy Covid virus is under control. We are creating a bond rooted in our shared DNA. Mom's ironing board still sits in tribute. While I now understand the cause of my strained attitude towards ironing, my linen shirts remain wrinkled.

An Astounding and Stimulating Trip

JEFFREY PEACOCK

I n my travels around the world, I have seen, tasted, or experienced many incredibly wonderful things. However, my trip to Vietnam in 1963 was the most stimulating and quite unusual in unexpected ways. You, too, may have undoubtedly enjoyed numerous such experiences, but today's tale will delve into the more uncommon side of international travel.

My travel to Vietnam as a young, newly commissioned second lieutenant was certainly exciting. The heat, hustle, and hectic activity of Saigon were an astounding experience.

Reality, however, hit home when I was assigned to serve as a liaison officer to several South Vietnamese artillery units. My job was to help evaluate their combat effectiveness and what, if any, training and equipment they would require to be on a par with similar American military units.

The travel to the units was often difficult due to poor, rutted roads. These were all too often simply quagmires of viscous mud or stifling dust. Each trip was anxiety-inducing due to the possibility of roadside bombs or sniper fire from the nearby forest.

The color and variety of the Vietnamese countryside were fascinating, when not being fired upon. Had these travels been for tourism, they would have been edifying and stimulating in a positive way. However, the stimulation was mostly negative, with each trip possibly being the last.

Each visit to a Vietnamese artillery unit entailed days of boring preparation and travel to remote locations. While visiting with the Vietnamese military, I was offered culinary delicacies, which it would have been insulting to refuse. The most repellant meal consisted of congealed pigs' blood and peanuts. This feast cost me a week of heavy-duty antibiotics and numerous visits to the slit trenches. Although the stench of the latrines was nauseating, the swarming, buzzing flies did not seem to mind. The huge cockroaches, who, in my opinion, were members of a North Vietnamese chemical warfare unit, were particularly annoying given their desire to crawl where they were not welcome.

During one visit to an artillery unit near the Cambodian border, an element of the North Vietnamese Army (NVA) attacked South Vietnamese Ranger companies conducting interdiction of NVA infiltration routes into South Vietnam. The artillery unit I was visiting provided three days of fire support to the rangers. The unit itself was attacked on the second night of my visit but managed to withstand the assault, although NVA sappers broke through barbed-wire defenses on two occasions.

After the firefight, I remember standing in a hot, drenching rain, tired to the bone, weeping with frustration as my ice cream melted in my mess kit. I was exhausted, suffering from post-combat letdown and the utter silliness of the American supply unit from which I had requested a resupply of ammunition expended by the Vietnamese unit. The American logistical company had shipped ice cream and soda rather than artillery shells because "the Vietnamese needed moral support!"

Amazing! My time served in Vietnam was both "stimulating" and "astounding," but I prefer that today's travels involve better cuisine, cleaner bathrooms, and far less excitement.

Resist

LAURIE LEINONEN

The phone rings. Caller ID appears on the TV screen. I let it ring. It is really hard for me to just let it ring. I have always been a compulsive phone answerer. My kids would say, "Just let it ring!" But I couldn't. Maybe it came from growing up in a large family in a small town with party lines and not much privacy. You kind of dialed, but not really. The operator would put it through. It was a big deal when we got our own house lines. With these long cords, you could move around even while tethered to the wall or the base. There was major excitement when the Princess Wall Phone came out.

The phone rings again. I check caller ID on the phone. I let it ring. I really want to answer, but I know it's best that I don't. It's painful to let it ring and ring. I practically have to sit on my hands to keep from reaching out for it. I am coming up with reasons why I am not answering. I could be outside getting the mail or walking the dog. That helps calm me down. And lessen the guilt. We can't always be available.

The phone rings again while I am walking the dog. I check caller ID and know I will not answer it. I come up with more rationalizations. The battery is dead. I left it at home. There may or may not be a message to check later. At least the messages go straight to the phone, so I don't have to listen to them until I want to.

If I want to.

It's hard resisting the call, literally, of the phone, let alone the caller.

It has taken me more than a few months to come to the realization that it really will *not* matter *if I don't answer.* But it still bothers me, not just because I feel I am ignoring someone I care deeply about but because of the fear that something could be wrong.

One time, the calls came later in the night. I am able to ignore the first two, but by the third I can no longer resist for fear that something *is* wrong. Of course, nothing is really wrong. It is the same call I get many times a day. *There is someone here I don't know, sitting at my dining room table. Just sitting there. I don't want him here. I don't need this! I am fine by myself. I don't drive. I have turned off the stove. This is ridiculous! I am going to tell him to go home. That a friend is coming over to take me to dinner, so he doesn't need to be here. Can you do that?* No. The guilt and sadness wash over me, even knowing that in less than ten minutes, the sadness will be gone and there will be no memory of it . . . *for her.*

On Disappointment

BETH SHAW

The most memorable and ultimately instructive disappointment of my life occurred when I was barely five years old. Like everyone, I've suffered many disappointments over the years, but even after all this time, one memory springs immediately to mind as I contemplate writing on this topic. This was the Christmas morning when I found a Nancy Lee doll under our Christmas tree, rather than the Shirley Temple doll I had asked Santa for.

I remember vividly how shocked I was, and how confused I was about how to react. I should be grateful for the gift, but it wasn't what I'd asked for, desperately desired, or expected. To be sure, Nancy Lee dolls look a lot like Shirley Temple dolls. I'm not sure why my mother chose Nancy Lee. Maybe she cost a little less, or maybe because, with her dark hair and eyes, she looked more like me than the Shirley Temple doll did. To most people, any difference between the two dolls would seem minute. To me, it was cataclysmic. I recall clearly expressing my disappointment, then sensing my mother's surprise and hurt feelings (though, supposedly, the doll came from Santa), and then trying to cover my feelings and be a good sport about it.

As it turned out, I quickly grew to love Nancy Lee. She was the only doll I ever owned. I didn't "play dolls" much, but I got her up and dressed her every morning and put her back every night in her cardboard box bed. In later years, I practiced my design and sewing skills on an extensive wardrobe for her. She sat on my dresser until I was in my mid-forties when, sadly, she suffered a fall that cracked her pretty little composition head in two and she left my life.

I think that the dramatic turnaround in my feelings about this doll taught me the most valuable lesson of my life: We don't always get what we want, but that can turn out to be okay, and sometimes, may be better than what we wanted in the first place. It taught me not necessarily to take disappointment lying down but to give reality a chance.

A major disappointment in my adult life was—for quite a while—not having children of my own. For many years, I struggled with feelings of loss and deprivation, regret at not having what most women have, and missing out on the closeness that procreation entails. But there was always a part of me that saw there were some pluses to my situation, and I took advantage of them. I have developed some beautiful, unique relationships with other people's children, and when stepchildren entered my life, I was able to welcome and appreciate them unconditionally. I was also aware that some very rewarding paths I was taking, such as the pursuit of a Ph.D. and traveling the world, were made possible or were greatly facilitated by my childless state.

So, is disappointment a bad or a good thing? It is certainly painful and can, if we let it, dampen our spirits and threaten our faith, but it happens to everyone. It need not be crippling, and it may, if one can move past it, open windows onto unexplored pathways and unimagined opportunities.

The Deep Blue Sea

LUELLEN RAMEY

I was excited to arrive in St. Petersburg, Florida, to crew on a sail to Havana.

The event was the 1997 Havana Cup. Though we were not racing, a number of sailboats, ours among them, were being allowed to follow leisurely behind the racing boats. Our boat and crew had permission to enter Cuba because we were taking sorely needed medical supplies and wheelchairs aboard. As part of this delivery, we were allowed to dock in Hemingway Marina for a week.

Our sailboat, *Marcus*, was forty-two-foot Cabo Rico, very woody and beautiful, and designed for blue water sailing. Marc Kaufman, a friend, was its owner and captain. Heather and Adam and me and my partner, Dave, who'd flown down from Michigan, were the crew. We were looking forward to a sail that we anticipated would take about sixty hours.

Leaving Tracy's Cove Marina in St. Pete on March 24th, the weather was a sailor's dream—warm and sunny with a good breeze and clear blue sky. We adjusted the sails, then just enjoyed moving gently toward our heading. Three playful dolphins followed behind our boat for some time. There was a beautiful orange sunset over the water. We took turns napping and on watch over the starry night as our boat glided toward our destination. We were far into the Gulf, no longer seeing the coastline of Florida or any other land.

The sunrise over the water was gorgeous. Then, as the day wore on, the clouds moved in, and we knew we were in for rain. Not a problem. We were on a seaworthy boat and had our rain gear. I went to the V-berth in the bow to nap before my watch. As darkness descended, rain began pelting down, and the sea became very rough. The boat was pitching and creaking. I got up and helped the other crew members to tightly secure everything in place. No storage space could be opened now.

Below deck is the easiest place to get seasick, and sure enough, two of our crew members were already sick. It was time to close the cabin and secure ourselves with tethers to the main stanchion in the cockpit so there was no risk of man overboard. We would have to ride the storm out like this. There was no place for shelter.

So there we were—Adam at the wheel because even the captain was seasick—and two of us on the hard seats on each side, port and starboard. The high waves caused the hull of the boat to rise, then slap down. The wind howled and moaned as rain came down in sheets. Shackles, shrouds, and stays clanked against the mast. Occasionally, a rogue wave would break over the boat, drenching us and putting the entire boat under water for a moment. Even with our rain gear, we were soaked to the skin. Dave and I gripped each other's hand as we held on for dear life with the other hand. We prayed the boat would hold together.

After what seemed like hours, the storm passed. We could finally see land ahead! We hoisted the Cuban flag to the top of the mast, the Stars and Stripes below, and entered the channel to Hemingway Marina.

A Curious and Quirky DNA

JACK WILLIAMSON

"Remember, he is a FOMA dog." These were the parting words from our new puppy's breeder as we drove away from her home. Little did I know how quickly I would discover them to be so true Gus, our ten-week-old, cute as Christmas, puppy, and how his FOMA (Fear of Missing Anything) label might fit me too.

FOMA is both a wonderful and an annoying characteristic. It happens when anything in Gus's world changes, from as little as someone leaving a room, to the crashing of a falling pan, to the smell of fresh popcorn. He stays alert for anything that changes or anything that he believes needs his help or attention.

Now, after five years of his loving and curious presence in our home, I am beginning to admit that I too may have a streak of FOMA as a part of my personality.

- I like the changing seasons and living in Colorado that affords this joy.

- I am a news junky, curious to know what is changing in our world.

- I like talking with all sorts of people, learning about what makes others tick . . . and me too.

- As a foodie, I find it interesting how even the slightest of changes in a recipe can make a dish taste better, or worse.

Reading provides windows into new thoughts, propelling me, at times, to change my mind from the insights of others and differing points of view.

Typically, I have prided myself on welcoming and adjusting to change. Like most people, whether by chance, choice, or crisis, I have navigated some heady currents of change. Learning to move from feeling like the victim of unwelcome changes to becoming a thriver has been a goal—often a difficult, ongoing, and conscious process.

I believe a purposeful and meaningful life is realized through the process of paying attention and adjusting to major and minor changes over a lifetime. Divorce, single-parenting, cancer diagnosis, coming out of my own sexuality closet, moving and living around the world, aging and deaths of family members, friends, and pets—these and a myriad of other changes, both large and small, have fed my FOMA curiosity. When I feel good about consciously adjusting to these and other changes, I feel awake, alive, and mostly joyful. When I am able to connect with others who are traversing their own challenges of change, I know I am not alone and feel connected.

Gus, as an energetic five-year-old canine companion has gifted me with his FOMA DNA, teaching me how to appreciate and embrace the traces of my own FOMA personality.

Moving and Friendships

RICHARD MANSBACH

F riends or new adventure? That dichotomy has followed me for half my life. It wasn't until my forties that I emphasized friendships, and I see now how nourishing to my soul close friends are, and I treasure these relationships. Wasn't always that way.

I nominally made friends growing up. What I mean is I must have subconsciously known I would be moving to another city soon and did not hold much of a connection to them once I did move.

'Oh well," I would say. "There will be new friends in the next city." This was because my dad kept changing jobs and then relocating every three to four years. I was an only child and found the moves exciting, and yet, there was an unsettling undercurrent of fear starting over, alone. The fact that I was outgoing, friendly, and kind did help smooth the way for new connections.

The move that did not give a warm glow of excitement was going to Birmingham, Alabama, during the civil rights movement. Separate drinking fountains, separate seating for movie theaters, and separate seating on buses, where the sign declaring "whites only" was moved back as more whites boarded. I was in junior high and don't remember making any friends there. In fact, I was terrified. I remember sitting next to a large man-child who told me he would meet a "n…" on the front steps of the school with a hammer if they tried to enter.

I also learned from my dad that animals were nothing to get attached to. Moving from Pittsburgh to Birmingham, he said we had to leave behind our Great Dane, which was excruciating, like the leading lady in an opera taking twenty minutes to die. Looking back, I feel that caused me more anguish than leaving my friends.

Thankfully, that changed once I left home. I am exceptionally attached to the cats in my life, having taken them across an international border and several state lines.

Along with a new adventure comes a new location, and I have discovered as an adult, how a place resonates can make it a *home* or simply a waystation, similar to kissing like you mean it, or simply a peck on the cheek.

Reading Carlos Castaneda taught me the importance of place. He was told by his mentor, Don Juan, to sense the power rock he had placed under the porch, and Carlos spent all day sitting here and there before he found his "place on the porch."

Boulder County, Colorado, is my place on the porch, as discovered by me living here for the third time. In combination with the close, spiritual friendships my wife and I have fostered friendships, and location and new adventure may have finally melded together.

I am home.

My Left Foot

MARINA FLORIAN

I have a new manila folder on my desk titled "My Left Foot." It doesn't contain a renowned autobiography or film script, but rather a dossier of X-rays and an MRI report. Having torn several ligaments in my foot five months ago during the "March for Our Lives" in Denver, I can identify with the phrase, "No good deed goes unpunished."

This injury prevents me from taking leisurely walks and has ended my once-daily routine of a late-afternoon hike with my husband and golden retriever. I have added new activities to fill in the empty spaces and take numerous precautions to safeguard my foot. I am cognizant that healing takes time and am reluctantly practicing patience.

But, I wonder, *How is this affecting me?* Now, at the reasonably young age of sixty-six, this infirmity occupies the bulk of my daily thought processes. Formerly, when my desk was at a university or at a bank, my full attention was on the next new project, its schedule, and multiple impending deadlines. I had colleagues with whom I discussed what I believed were crucial and demanding issues.

Now retired, I have no pressure to oversee projects, define a budget, or troubleshoot construction issues gone bad. So, I dwell on my left foot.

I am not like Christy Brown, the author of *My Left Foot*, whose foot was his route to achieving greatness and crafting a life. Instead, my foot complaint makes me feel like an iceberg, slowly melting, heading in the direction of oblivion.

All our lives, we are building, creating. Then, as we reach a certain age, we are headed in the opposite direction. I have only felt this way since I hurt my foot, when my routines were altered, when I became barred from my daily, ingrained patterns. Perhaps this is only a temporary inconvenience, and I know it could be much worse.

Yet, I feel it is the beginning of another life, and my trajectory seems to be shifting. I wonder, *Why did this happen to me less than a year after I retired?* I am sure this is a question for all of us who are aging, and unable to live as we once did. I hope that I might someday resolve my foot issue.

Meanwhile, I continue to explore new patterns and experiment with alternative activities. Life used to be a guaranteed plethora of rousing and thrilling events, yet now I am learning how to give in, to accept a new course. As per the wise observation by the fictitious Count Alexander Rostov in "*A Gentleman in Moscow,*" I realize that as life changes, new subtleties emerge.

> Alexander Rostov was neither scientist or sage: but at the age of sixty-four he was wise enough to know that life does not proceed by leaps and bounds. It unfolds. At any given moment, it is the manifestation of a thousand transitions. Our faculties wax and wane, our experiences accumulate, and our opinions evolve—if not glacially, then at least gradually. Such that the events of an average day are as likely to transform who we are as a pinch of pepper is to transform a stew. ("*A Gentleman in Moscow*" by Amor Towles)

Girlfriends

SUSAN JOSEPHS

When my husband, kids, and I moved to Connecticut, I felt like I'd been dropped into Never Never Land. There were no kindred spirits anywhere in sight. One day, Gisela, who cared for my son after preschool, invited her next-door neighbor for coffee so we could meet. Catherine and I recognized each other immediately, becoming fast friends moments into our introduction. She asked me my birthdate. I took a gamble, hoping I was answering her *real* question:

"I'm a Taurus with a Pisces moon, and Leo rising."

She didn't miss a beat.

"Wow, we're Sun-Moon opposites! I'm a Scorpio with a Virgo moon and Scorpio rising."

Never Never Land wasn't going to be so completely dreary after all. We have the important stuff in common, even though we're quite different. We talk every day and share things that no one else knows. Life is more bearable because of our friendship.

She's from the Bronx. I'm from Manhattan. We're both of Sicilian heritage. She's Catholic. I'm Jewish. She has six children and raised two of her sister's. My daughter and son are the same ages as her only daughter and youngest son.

Through Catherine, I met other crazy women trapped in the suburbs. I don't blame the suburbs for making us crazy, but I'm sure it didn't help. When our kids went to elementary school, Catherine and I, and a bunch of girls would meet several mornings a week at Jacqueline's Restaurant for breakfast. We could laugh at the dumbest stuff. Suburb therapy.

Over eggs, toast, and coffee, we'd plan our illustrious futures, fantasizing about crazy careers as psychics, past-life regression therapists, and—who can even remember. We had such harebrained plans. Then we'd help each other sort out the little problems of our current, slightly boring lives and, of course, the *Big Picture* details too.

After breakfast, we'd return to the realities of life in the burbs: grocery shopping, greeting our kids after school, tennis, baseball, dance class, making dinner, homework help, and taking care of our houses, husbands, and aging parents while dreaming what we'd be when we grew up. I couldn't make dinner without a call to Catherine.

We've shared graduations from preschool, elementary school, high school, and college. We've survived hairstyle changes (her hair's curly, mine is straight), financial difficulties, children and husband crises, menopause, and hormone therapy. She took. I didn't. We even figured out how to leave a hairdresser and come back a year later without too much embarrassment.

We both had parathyroidectomies and obsessed over the best way to banish the scars. We philosophized that the surgeries had opened our throat chakras, and now our voices would be heard. So far, we're still the only ones listening to each other.

Astrology is our metaphor for understanding life and its curveballs. We know that motherhood challenges us and shapes who we are since our Cancer North Node's primary lesson is learning to nurture.

We spend a lot of time putting *white light* around our children, hoping this ritual will keep them safe. And we just keep talking to each other. It helps. My daughter calls us the "vague psychics," but whenever she calls to ask my counsel, she always ends with, "Mommy, ask Catherine to *tune in.*"

I went to college. Catherine didn't. Her knowledge is raw and intuitive. Mine depends more on coaxing things into rational trappings. I trust her insights over anyone I know. We'll bounce just about anything off of each other, grappling for hours over a dream and its interpretation or a life decision as though we have control! So, while we're always giving and taking advice, we're also trying to answer the questions of the universe at the same time.

We were our mothers' primary caregivers, Grandma Meatball (hers) and Queen Esther (mine), helping each other make decisions about their end-of-life care and deal with the impossibility of *the loss.* With both of our precious, amazing, difficult, and demanding mothers gone, we stepped, oh-so-cautiously, into their shoes, becoming the matriarchs of our own families.

These days, we deal with memory loss, hoping one of us remembers what the other one has forgotten. How will we know?

And our roles as mothers are always changing, so together, we're trying to adapt. As adults, they need our occasional emotional cradling as well as our meatballs and spaghetti. (She calls it gravy. I call it sauce.) And we need a subtlety in our nurturing that wasn't required when they were younger. We're still learning how to mother. As long as we can talk, we'll figure it out.

We know we'll make it through this phase and into the next. We're always just a phone call and a laugh away. We can handle whatever life hands us. We may be Sun-Moon opposites, but we're girlfriends, and that friendship makes life's bumps and grooves manageable. If not, we'll talk.

The Church of My Childhood

LAURA K. DEAL

L ast Saturday, I entered the church of my childhood for the first time
since 1989. The First United Methodist Church of Fort Collins, built
in 1963, has beautiful stained glass in squares, rectangles, and paral-
lelograms. The blue, teal, pink, and gold panes caught my attention
when I was a child, seated in the front pew with my family. I looked for
patterns in the placement of the colors, but there were none.

I enjoyed the music, especially when the whole congregation
sang, because then I could stand up and use my voice rather than sitting quietly in what was usually a scratchy polyester dress, tights, and
shiny black leather shoes. I dutifully got up and filed out with the other
children when it was time to go to our Sunday school classrooms. We
walked through the hallway with the painting of Jesus, looking benev-
olently down at us with his white skin and light brown hair. In our
almost exclusively white church and white town, such whitewashing
of history was the norm.

I learned that Jesus loved children, though I was unclear on
how exactly that related to me. At home, my parents weren't overtly
religious, but went to church for the community and because it was
socially expected. We did say grace before dinner, a quick, "Father,

we thank thee for this food; please bless it to our use, and us to thy service. Amen." They were just words, syllables that flowed from my mouth before we could drink our milk and eat our vegetables, meat, and potatoes. Grace was merely the starting point through a process that, if I could eat everything on my plate, led to dessert.

None of that fed my spiritual yearnings. I wanted to know why I was born to the parents I was, in the town I was, to live in a house and go to school. I knew there were children in other parts of the world who suffered from hunger, even famine, and who lived in conditions much more primitive than a new house with a furnace and running water. I wanted to understand why I'd been chosen for this life and not another. The odds seemed astronomical.

My true sanctuary was the big, blue Colorado sky. I lay on the neatly mown grass in the backyard and stared up at it, wondering why I thought dreams were important and meaningful and my very intelligent parents regarded them as the random firings of a sleeping brain. I wanted meaning more than anything, but I never found it in the church.

In 1989, I attended my grandmother's funeral in the church and then had no reason to be there until last weekend. Now an incredible pipe organ fills the front of the sanctuary, which my aunt was instrumental, as a lay leader, in obtaining. We listened to the hymns played on that organ. I longed to sing but couldn't because of the pandemic. The music filled the sanctuary, and I prayed, in my un-Methodist way, that my aunt's soul would be at peace.

Life on the Margin of Error

PEGGY WALLIS

> Our errors are surely not such awfully solemn things. In a world where we are so certain to incur them in spite of all our caution, a certain lightness of heart seems healthier than this excessive nervousness on their behalf.
>
> —William James, *"The Will To Believe"*

O ften it seems that I exist on the margin of error—that blurred line that separates the moral high ground from the downslope of many mistaken beliefs and possible errors. Shrouded in mist, it is a narrow, twisted path that has me carefully step over rocks and roots as my mind jumps from side to side, from "I know" to "I thought I knew," and back again. For there is no certainty here; only people who are certain. And I am not one of them.

My father was a man who believed in certainty: that the world was an orderly place and that the path was clear and straight. He was certain that people were basically honest, marriage was a contract not to be broken, hard work was rewarded, and the Dodgers would never leave Brooklyn. There was no margin of error for him; no fretting about possible mistakes. Even after his marriage ended, his business associates were not scrupulously honest, and the Dodgers moved to Los Angeles, he remained certain that the world was orderly and predictable. His disappointments and mistakes, if any, were never shared.

My husband is a neurosurgeon, certain of his skill and ability to heal. "To cut is to cure," is a surgeon's mantra, and cut they do. With little margin for error, cuts must be precise, and extreme care must be taken to avoid catastrophic mistakes. For no one wants to hear the words "close enough" in matters of the brain. There is no place for him on the downslope of mistake or error, the path that leads from sunny certainty into the mist of doubt.

I think of both of these men, the touchstones of my life, as my plane touches down in Portland, and I see the silver streaks of rain running down the window. They are so different, my father and husband, and yet so alike in their certainty—a lovely mixture of kindness and arrogance.

My uncertainty, my flight from possible error, has made me tired, and I am in need of a lightness of heart. Here to visit my daughter, my body is tense with anticipation and needing release. A weekend is too short a time to fully reconnect, and yet, I will try to make it enough. She is a mental health clinician and often treats me like a patient, challenging me fiercely when I say something thoughtless or unkind, leaving me dizzy and lurching from "I know" to "I thought I knew" while wilting under her relentless demand for honesty. Yet, it is this fierce honesty that pushes me toward the elusive moral high ground and away from that perilous, erroneous downslope.

I stand on the sidewalk, zipping up my rain jacket, as I check my phone for messages. Scanning the road for her arrival, I notice other passengers, looking travel-worn and waiting for their loved ones with eager faces. And then I spot her car, fifteen-years-old and sporting dents that she was too busy to have repaired. With a smile, I run to place my suitcase in the trunk, knowing that there is no margin of error here. There is only love.

Fractal Hibernation

SARAH MASSEY-WARREN

Unfortunately, nature is very much a now-you-see-it, now-you-don't affair.

—Annie Dillard

"I feel like a candle without a wick," confesses Sasha. She and I tarp our neighboring gardens against the onslaught of unseasonal September snow. Six damn inches will smash our plants. We snip my sunflowers—bouquets for all. Phoebe, her ten-month-old daughter, clings to Sasha with a monkey grip. Sasha and Nick welcomed their baby a year ago, right before the pandemic and winter hit hard, magnifying the deep, dark reaches of parenthood.

Now-you-see-it.

Nothing lets loose but winter, come early.

The landscape rocks on fluctuating waves, seventy degrees one week, ten degrees the next. The water pouring from the hose just seven days prior pools in frozen buckets, encasing the oak tree roots. My thoughts plunge, shuddering into the winter mercury.

The pandemic transforms the university into a cold, hollow core. Student faces freeze into fractal boxes; they populate my computer screen. Zombie thoughts lock in Zoom gloom. Poltergeists abduct my hard drive.

The rubber tree keels over on the kitchen table. Having outgrown its perch, it pushes off the ceiling and leaps. Ten years ago, I rescued it from Home Depot. The seedling had two leaves. Now, it needs a new pot, and a new home. It skirts my floorboards, and my ceiling corners, looking for the winter light only found on the kitchen table.

My house drifts in ghosts. I watch the rubber tree and wish. Where did the sunflowers go?

Now-you-don't.

I met my husband through a poem I wrote for his art publication, *Art Throb*. My daughters and I lived alone in this house that only he wanted. So much for poetry.

Writing and children find you on their terms.

Twenty-six inches of snow bury Boulder. Nick steam-shovels his sidewalk and mine. A snowsuit bubble trails him. Phoebe, now walking, toddles in his wake, the Corgi, Pickles, in hers, like winter growth. Sasha breathes crystalized cloud blossoms that linger.

In Texas, trees hibernate twice—in summer from the heat, in winter from the cold. Live Oaks and Osage Orange reach laterally for decades, stunted like dwarves, weaving like spiders. Their roots expand unseen, north to Oklahoma and south to the Gulf of Mexico. Maybe that's what thought can do when hope grows cold. Maybe the heart follows.

The temperature hits minus ten. I lie fallow. I ditch the frozen students and cleanse with four loads of laundry. For the first time, I watch "*Fiddler on the Roof*." Tevya discovers that females have brains and wills, against a backdrop of an Imperialist Russian pogrom exiling Tevya's Jewish community from their ancient Russian village of Anatevka. Uprooted in winter, they leave as whole.

The university cancels spring break. Hoping to revive my frozen students, I tell them that we are taking a two-week Zoom hiatus. No screens. At last, they smile and almost bloom. Hope hovers.

Now-you-see-it.

The land lies frozen. A wick lurks beneath, awaiting a flame. Next to the sunflower seeds.

Rocky Mountain High

BETH SHAW

S oft blooms of white light exploded behind banks of puffy clouds in the night sky. We drifted out onto the porch to watch these sudden but gentle apparitions, one after the other. None of us had ever seen anything like it.

I shared these magical moments and so many more during the three days I spent at the Rocky Mountain YMCA Camp with about thirty former Peace Corps volunteers and their partners. The volunteers had all served in Tunisia between 1983 and 1985. We came from all over the country. Some of us had known each other fairly well almost forty years ago but hadn't seen each other since; some had kept closely in touch; a few of us had never actually met or spoken before, but our shared two years of Peace Corps experience and of life in Tunisia at that particular time created a sense of familiarity and community for us.

Besides the literal 8,000+ foot altitude, the amazing natural light show, and the clear Colorado blue or star-studded skies, most of the highs we experienced were in the connections and conversations that kept happening. As the three of us were getting dressed one morning, our casual banter turned spontaneously into extensive, intense narrations of our respective marriage experiences. I knew one of these women only slightly and the other not at all, but by the end of an hour, we knew a great deal about each other.

With Hichem Feti, who had been one of our Tunisian language instructors in 1983 and who joined us in Colorado, we enjoyed an impromptu session of *molokhia* recipe and memory sharing. *Molokhia* is a sauce made from jute mallow leaves. It looks a lot like dirty motor oil, and you either love it (I do) or hate it.

Probably the most significant conversation for me was one that took place the second night of the reunion between me, Jim, a volunteer I had known fairly well in Tunisia but had lost touch with, and Nina, a volunteer I had met before and admired but had never really talked with. Jim, like me, had lost his spouse fairly recently after a long period of caregiving, and Nina had recently lost her father and has become the main caregiver for her mother. Our conversation touched on life, death, grief, and consciousness, and promises to continue in coming days.

This reunion was a very different experience from my attendance a few weeks ago at a wedding where I was cast in the role of *little old lady*. At this recent gathering, I was treated as a peer—a member of a group that had shared similar experiences nearly forty years ago. Although I am more than twenty years older than many of the Tunisia volunteers, the age difference seemed irrelevant. They're now in their sixties or early seventies, facing many of the same issues and asking many of the same questions I am. But perhaps the most exciting aspect of this event for me was my ability to participate and enjoy it fully as a newly single person. This gathering renewed my confidence in myself as a social being and was a high point for me in this current phase of life.

The Finger

LAURIE LEINONEN

I have four brothers, ages ranging from sixty-five to seventy-seven. I am the only girl and the middle child. Every once in a while, we get into an email exchange.

Recently, one of my brothers took his two adult daughters to Finland. He had read a book called *Deep River* about Finnish immigrants in southwestern Washington State, and the men in the book reminded him of our father.

My father was born in Leadville, Colorado. My grandfather had emigrated to the United States from Finland to work in the Climax molybdenum mine. The Finnish miners were the lowest of the low in Leadville. They lived in a shanty town called Finntown, just past Stringtown, where the mule drivers resided. When the mine shut down, nothing was left to indicate Finntown ever existed. There is a marker for Stringtown, though.

Our father ultimately grew up in Vancouver, Washington, moving as a young child with his parents and other relatives to join a growing and welcoming Finnish community. He graduated from high school, surviving the Great Depression, just as World War II was taking shape. Times were hard and money scarce, so he worked whatever jobs he could find—riding the rails and following jobs from Alaska to Colorado and back to Washington. Logging, mining, salmon fishing—he did whatever he could to earn money to send home and save for college. He eventually enrolled at Oregon State University and was a big man on campus: strong and handsome, the president of his fraternity, an outstanding athlete. and an engineering student. When the war broke out, he was offered a job at Boeing in what was considered a necessary deferment to support the war effort.

As my brothers read *Deep River*, other reminiscences of our father began to emerge, one of which was how he had lost the tip of one of his little fingers. One brother said it was a logging accident, while another was certain it was setting a dynamite blast. I chimed in with what I remembered as a little girl. We lived in a house above Puget Sound with a trail we would take down to the water to wriggle onto logs as they lolled and rolled about in the waves. Bainbridge Island was off in the distance. Pop told me he lost the tip of his finger while swimming to the island—he was bitten off by some sea creature. He fought it off, of course, and made it safely to shore.

In the flurry of responses to the Finger story, one brother questioned the veracity of my story. He felt it necessary to counter it with another, more detailed mining episode. Funny how sometimes there is a need to be right as opposed to simply sharing these memories. The idea that anyone would think I believed mine was a true story was a bit of a head scratcher. It was simply a sweet, quasi-scary tale told by a father to a young child snuggled up on his lap, inquisitively examining his hands and fingers.

Grandmom's Challenge

JANAT HOROWITZ

My heart feels broken this evening; it seemed like it was going to be so much fun. I told myself that my two granddaughters and I camping for a week at the Oregon Country Fair would be a blast for them. I've been going there for over twenty years and know how much fun it can be. It appears that I'm wrong about that. I know they adore me, but they're teenagers now with minds of their own. One has swim lessons she doesn't want to miss, and the other's idea of being alone with me and away from her teen friends was a "no."

The Oregon Country Fair, formerly known as the Oregon Renaissance Faire, takes place each July near Eugene, Oregon. It began in 1969, has 50,000 visitors daily, and there are 4,000 people who work the fair. The land that the Fair sits on is only used once a year, and much of the year it's under water as the river that runs through it overflows. The land feels sacred. The old, craggy trees, which hold each of the fair booths, have moss hanging from them—it's magical. The booths are built to fit into nature and not to stand out, so that one walks on dirt paths and comes upon a booth here and there.

The Fair is more than a good time; it's a community where people celebrate, work together, and laugh at our outrageous costumes. It's like a scene out of *Alice-in-Wonderland*. Patrons come and learn the latest ways to work for the earth, dance to live music, shop for handmade whatevers, and watch vaudeville skits. With multiple performance stages, it is a wonderful, hilarious, and educational adventure.

The Fair publicly is a daytime-only event, and it's not easy to get a night pass; one has to "know someone." My dear friend on the inside was able to get my granddaughters passes. Walking around the grounds at night, you find pockets of people singing, playing music, or laughing together.

I'm so sad that my granddaughters don't see what a rare gift I'm offering. These kids, who don't know what life is like without their cell phones, could hop away from modern life for a few days and experience a hobbit's world. It's a world without electricity, one that has wood heated showers. It changes your life to see such possibilities and a fun-loving, playful community.

I guess it's just not for my granddaughters now. The story I told myself was that these two teens would absolutely love going with me. It's hard to come up with a new story like "They're getting older and hanging out with friends is the most important thing to them; they love me as much as always but aren't interested in expanding their vistas the way I want them to." I guess I'm just an old hippie.

Unexpected Grace

LUELLEN RAMEY

M y friend, Vicky, lost her beloved cat, Choclo, recently. Talking with her about the death of her cat brought back a memory of the death of one of my cherished cats, Deva. Named for an Eastern term for God, Deva was a short-haired ginger cat, very mellow and affectionate. At home, he was my shadow, right there with me.

I was in graduate school in Gainesville, Florida. Deva and I had recently moved from a one-bedroom apartment into a four-bedroom house with three roommates. Deva was getting out often, but it seemed okay, as he would come when I called. There was a neighborhood park behind our house, and he liked to go and explore and sit in the grass and watch the birds and whatever else was going on. I was taking a full load of classes and working. I didn't have the time to carefully monitor his whereabouts. And it didn't seem like it would be fair to him to shut him in my bedroom for many hours at a time.

One day I came home, called him, but he didn't come. I went out looking for him and soon found him dead on the ground in the part of the park where he liked to hang out. Dry blood was visible from his open mouth. I was shocked to find him like this. I was on my knees, petting him and crying over him, when a man came up and saw what was happening. He summed up the situation, and in a gentle voice, he said that it looked to him as though my kitty had gotten into rat poison. We talked a little and he volunteered to help me bury Deva. He said he'd go to his house, get something to wrap him in, and bring a shovel and his car. We could go out to his friend's property at the edge of town to bury the cat. A few minutes later, he was back with a burlap bag, and I gently wrapped my cat.

It was drizzling as he dug the hole, and I lovingly put Deva in. I took the shovel and moved the dirt back in on top of him, crying while I did. We finished and the man dropped me off back at my house.

I was so focused on my kitty that I paid little attention to the man. I had never seen him before; I didn't know his name, and never saw him again. He was likely a neighbor, but I don't know. He understood my loss and offered his help. My intuition immediately took him to be sincere, which I was able to accept. Later, and even now, when I think about it, he seems almost angelic. He just appeared in my time of need, helped me, and disappeared.

Sustaining Friendships

SUSAN JOSEPHS

've never been into diamonds. Friendships are my great treasures. All the chapters and layers of my life have been blessed with priceless friends. Friendships have sculpted, influenced, healed, and comforted me, and have given me life-sustaining emotional richness.

Every few years, even though we're scattered around the country, I get together with friends I've had since childhood. In high school, we wore high heels, pencil skirts, and played grownup. We now laugh unabashedly, seeing the child in each other. One is still the zaniest, another the brightest, another the most literary, and one of us, the most political. After graduation, college took us in different directions. But when we four women get together, we reveal our deepest selves. Our diverging paths can't disturb our history.

Newly married in our twenties and thirties, my husband and I orchestrated our life plan. I began my first teaching job; my husband attended veterinary school; we had our two children. We tackled life's intensities with those friends who shared similarly ambitious goals. Friends made the journey easier to navigate as we all headed toward our careers and futures.

When raising our children, we connected with parents through our kids' school activities and competitive sports. We became friends, celebrated our kids' achievements, commiserated over their defeats, helped them flourish, and assuaged their emotional growing pains. We got each other through all the tough parts of parenting. Pizza parties always helped.

Retiring to Colorado, where my husband and I had met in college, we're now more carefree. We've become allies with our children, watching them take flight, no longer needing to be hovering parents preoccupied with protecting them. (Well, mostly.) Our move from "Back East" pulled us away from so many wonderful people. We try to preserve those bonds in order to remain whole. Despite our physical distance, I speak daily with my best friend, Catherine. We met in our late thirties. Our kids call us vague psychics. The secrets we share go into the "vault." Our forever friendship is deep, and our laughter is essential.

Now, in my seventies, I'm fascinated by how my new friends, as well as those I've known forever, have orchestrated their diverse lives. Elderhood offers freedom to nurture interests that went unfed while obligations commanded our time. New friendships add unanticipated fullness. Courageously aging allies share our highs and lows and seek insight into life's mysteries. We're distinct silhouettes piecing our puzzles together. Play is essential. So is inward reflection. So is rest.

While still healthy and free to travel, read, take classes, give back, and join others who share our zest for life, we relish friendships across multi-generations, ethnicities, and nationalities. My college roommate's daughter serendipitously bought the house next door. Reconnecting with her mother, giggling about our wild sixties rebelliousness,, we temporarily suspended fifty-eight years. Our separate histories never interfere with our memories.

There have been losses. When friends and family die, grief is palpable. Life's fragility, and the reminder of our mortality, is sobering. Recounting memories and discussing death and life's meaning sustains and enriches me. I am grateful for this precious fabric of friendships. Each treasured individual adds complexity, love, joy, and significance to my life.

I'll never miss those diamonds.

Flowers In Hell

PEGGY WALLIS

The Boardwalk at Coney Island is the longest and widest boardwalk in the world. It runs 2.7 miles from West 37th Street at the border of Coney Island and Sea Gate to Ocean Parkway in Brighton Beach. The Coney Island site was once the largest amusement area in the country at the turn of the century and was famed for its technological innovations at the time, such as electric lights and roller coasters, as well as a showcase of one of the world's most peculiar exhibits—a bizarre sideshow of rows of premature babies. My mother-in-law, who will turn 100 on October 14, was one of those babies.

Erin Merdy lived on Neptune Avenue in Coney Island. It was a three-block walk from the apartment that she lived in with her three children to the boardwalk. At nearly 1:00 a.m., draped in a bathrobe, she carried her three-month-old son in her arms. Her seven-year-old boy and four-year-old girl walked alongside, down across the sand to the water, as vulnerable as flowers in hell. And there, she ended her children's lives by drowning them in those dark waters. Leaving her children at the shoreline, she walked nearly two miles, soaking wet and without shoes. No roller coaster full of shrieking passengers viewed the passing of these babies. No crowds came to enjoy the sideshow, and no electric lights brightened their way. There was only the cold light of the moon, the cold sand, and the cruel water.

Erin Merdy faced murder charges in the drowning deaths of her three children. She was ordered held without bail during her bedside arraignment on Friday in the psychiatric ward at NYU Langone-Brooklyn Hospital. She had admitted "that she had hurt her children and that they were gone." Family members said that she suffered from mental health issues and may have been dealing with postpartum depression after the birth of her youngest child. The City Administration for Children's Services had at least two reports of neglect filed against her. A funeral was held Monday for her four-year-old daughter.

My husband is a member of a large and mostly happy family. He cannot understand how anyone could kill their own child. To him, each child is a blessing. He cannot comprehend the reality of an unwanted child. But I can. The universal myth of the loving mother who will sacrifice her life to protect her children is just that. A myth. When women are living at the edge of their sanity, with stressors most of us have never felt, the impulse to relieve that stress must be unbearable. And help is not on the way. We blame and shame women who cannot cope. Mental health intervention comes far too late. This family was known to some in the community. One child went to school. He played football. He told his coach he was always hungry. The family was facing eviction. Children's services knew about them. And nothing happened.

One day, Erin Merdy may fully realize what she has done and will have to live with that knowledge. And that, in her own way, she was also as vulnerable as a flower in hell. Surely people who turn premature babies into a sideshow for their own amusement can understand that.

The Collapse of the American Electrical Power Grid

JEFFREY PEACOCK

O ften called the world's biggest interconnected machine, the
American electrical power grid is exceedingly vulnerable to
attack and collapse. It consists of over seven thousand power plants,
more than fifty thousand separate substations, and two hundred thousand miles of transmission lines. Frankly, it is a miracle that it even
works. It is made up of more than three thousand different utilities
and is governed by a bewildering number of different state and fed-
eral organizations.

These entities barely communicate with each other. Much of the
infrastructure is over fifty years old, and some of it has been running
for one hundred years. The day-to-day operation of this complex
system involves an incredible balancing act requiring that supply and
demand be perfectly matched.

In 2003, the system had one of the biggest blackouts in our
history. Fifty million people were without power. Why? A tree branch
brushed a power line, and there should have been an alarm. However,
a software glitch caused a cascade of power failures!

If a simple act of nature can cause such a massive power outage, imagine the catastrophe that would result from a malicious, coordinated physical and cyber-attack. Blowing up a few strategic pieces of hardware would cause extensive damage, but the key to catastrophic collapse would be a successful attack on the SCADA system (Supervisory Control and Data Acquisition system). In other words, cyberwar launched by an enemy of the United States. Were a hacker able to place malware in the computer systems of American electric utility companies, we would be facing the possible collapse of our society.

Impossible? No, not even too difficult. Most of the critical electrical nodes run by our utility companies are guarded by nothing more than warning signs and wire fences. We have already seen hackers successfully attack sensitive military computer systems, to say nothing of the ramsomware attacks designed to disrupt our banking and business organizations.

The United States depends on electricity for almost every facet of our everyday lives. Food production, transportation, health care, eating, refrigeration and water supply. Our country is like a finely tuned watch—incredibly effective if every single gear turns properly. But if even one piece fails, we will witness a collapse of dystopian proportions. Industry and government experts have predicted such a collapse would have the same effect as a large-scale nuclear attack.

No electricity means no refrigeration, no heating, no water flowing, no gas being pumped, no lighting, no distribution of food, etc. Without electricity, hospitals cannot function, airports shut down, and so on. Let your imagination describe the chaos and panic that this would cause for our country.

What can you do to prepare: buy a two-year supply of MREs (meals ready to eat); stockpile medications, gas, water, and other necessities to survive in a dystopian world where it is every family for itself to fight for life's necessities.

The good news is that FINALLY, the government is beginning to focus on the vulnerability of our electric utility system. Unfortunately, there is enormous and long-standing resistance by our nation's electricity suppliers to upgrading the security of the electric power network. It may be years before our government and private industry undertake any significant improvements in the security of our electrical systems.

Friendship

MARY ANN PALIANI

The two golden retrievers trudged side by side, slowly, wearily along the shoulder of the heavily trafficked highway. They were panting heavily from extreme fatigue. Their fur was tangled and encrusted with mud. One limped very badly. They were in the middle of a life crisis. But they were confronting it together. Their behavior very simply, but eloquently, epitomized the meaning of friendship.

Aristotle has said a friend is "A single soul in two bodies." Best friends come in different sizes, shapes, genders, ethnicities—even species. But one thing is common to all: the individuals involved have each other's backs. Their focus is on the greater good of the other party.

I've had human friends. But one of my most cherished best friends was a dog named Jimmy. Jimmy and I came together when he first appeared on my doorstep one morning begging for food. I have no idea what power inexplicably led this big, black Labrador with an alpha male personality to me. But from the very beginning, we bonded in a very special way. It was as if we had a karmic, past-life connection. Perhaps it was his mission in this life to teach me the essence of friendship—mutual trust, loyalty, and support.

When Jimmy was with me, I knew no fear. I trusted him with my life! Memories of his loyalty and protectiveness toward me are like precious jewels, which will warm my heart and nurture my soul for the rest of my life. Let me share a couple with you.

About a month after he entered my life, we were walking in a deserted park in the early hours of an October morning. While I was standing there, waiting for Jimmy to collect the messages left in the grass and leaves by his canine and feline associates, someone knocked me to the ground. While I lay there dazed, Jimmy leaped into action. He grabbed the miscreant by the butt and detained her until I ordered him to let go. It turned out that my "attacker" was just a woman jogging around the park. Neither of us had seen each other in the pitch blackness of the 5:00 a.m. morning. But, in an instant, Jimmy decisively dealt with what he perceived was a threat to me. While the jogger's dog, also a black Lab, did nothing to intervene on her owner's behalf, Jimmy was loyal and protective.

Yet another example of his protectiveness occurred during a visit from a man who neither of us had previously met. My caller brought up an issue that required my going upstairs for some documents. I quickly jumped up from the couch and started climbing the stairs. Suddenly, I heard a scream. I thought to myself, *"Oh my God, Jimmy has attacked my visitor."* I spun around on the stairs. Jimmy was at my heels. When I returned to the living room, my guest explained that as soon as I had reached the stairs, Jimmy had shot across the living room like a black, ballistic missile. Then, like an Olympic gold medalist, he vaulted over my guest's arm, as he poured himself some tea from a carafe disturbing neither the man's arm, nor the carafe or the tea. Such was Jimmy's determination to be at my side. You might say Jimmy had a flair for the spectacular.

As he aged and physically deteriorated, it was my turn to support him in the unquestioning way he had taken care of me over the years. To me, the time, costs, and creative measures I subsequently undertook to accommodate Jimmy's disabilities were inconsequential. Trips to the CSU Veterinary Hospital in Fort Collins and to a veterinarian in the mountains who practiced alternative veterinary medicine were now just routine excursions. I had to maintain Jimmys quality of life for as long as possible.

Like the two golden retrievers, Jimmy and I trudged together along life's sometimes rough road. For fourteen years, we were at each other's sides—supporting each other, trusting each other, and caring for each other. We parted when Jimmy signaled that his mission in this life—to guide me through the profound experience of friendship—was accomplished. Then, it was time to say goodby.

A Cat's Tail

RICHARD MANSBACH

M y name is Zoey. I own a matched pair, male and female, of the *homo sapiens* species. I have been training them for over ten years and have modestly observed that they have come a long way since we were introduced.

Because they are larger than I am, it was important to develop trust first, so I hung out under their resting place so that I could observe them without being disturbed. With enough observational data, I determined they were good candidates for the next stage: contact training.

Being touched is a two-way street. I have observed how humans get pleasure from stroking me, but my pleasure resides in being stroked in the right way. You must take into account variables such as pressure, location, frequency of stroke, their sounds when applying strokes, and allowing me to fall asleep while still being petted. By twisting my body, I can guide their hands, but sometimes they are slow on the uptake to observe my desire to be petted differently on any given day. Oh, how important patience is.

The male, whom I call Q-Tip for his white hair, has been easy to train. In the morning, I let him know if he is derelict in responding quickly enough to my hunger impulse. Most times, he prioritizes my needs over his need to go to the bathroom.

I find time to meditate while Q-Tip does his Tai Chi. I lie close to his feet with my eyes in a soft gaze and my paws curled under my chin to enhance my chi. I have trained him not to step on me, which is important and contributes to the two-way trust we have developed.

When I want to play, I jump on the arm of a couch and signal to him, and he immediately runs into their resting place room and retrieves the ribbon I enjoy chasing. The activity keeps me fit and is naturally fun. I'm pleased that he seems to enjoy it as well. Consistent signals keep him engaged and trained. As they say, a happy Q-Tip makes for a happy cat.

The female keeps trying to hold me like a baby, which I detest, and I jump down at the first opportunity. But otherwise, she has a great lap to stretch out on with my head in a downward position. I honor her with my butt in her face to show my appreciation.

About my tail, it twitches, and if you pay close attention, it can tell you some things that will give signals as to my state of mind. This will be useful because when you are not focused on me, it is frankly annoying.

For example, I might be swishing slowly as I check out danger from the back. Your job is to continue petting me, but know that I'm not completely relaxed. A faster twitch means you aren't stroking in a pleasing way. Please tune in.

All in all, though, they're both doing a purrfect job and have my purr approval.

Food Extinction Coming

JANAT HOROWITZ

It is with fear, sadness, and the frustration of powerlessness that I share my recent research discoveries. Food can become extinct! We have heard for decades about animals going extinct, and tragically, that's become the norm. Recently, we heard that the last male white rhino died. Boom! That's the end of that species; only two females are left in the whole world.

But food? With global warming, crops like coffee are in trouble. In many coffee-growing regions, the higher humidity and warming temperatures are causing diseases and pests to thrive, and unpredictable temperatures and rainfall patterns are impacting harvest times and crop quality.

And that's not all. Wine is being affected for the same reasons at wineries. There may be a *"bouquet of ashtray"* in your future bottle of wine. Seafood will also be one of the foods most affected by climate change because of water pollution, increased water temperatures, and ocean acidification. Because of environmental changes, there will also be issues with chocolate, vanilla, potatoes, squash, tomatoes, avocados, strawberries, bananas, apples, prunes, and ginger.

Add almonds to that list. Growing one almond requires 1.1 gallons of water, and to grow a pound, it takes 1,900 gallons of water. The crazy thing about that is that other nuts all use roughly the same amount of water to grow as well, but the almond is in high demand now for its use as a milk alternative.

This all makes me wonder how people are going to eat and drink in the next two to three decades. Will life be as it was as portrayed in the 2006 science fiction comedy film, "Idiocracy," where Dr. Pepper rather than water flows through our pipes? I probably won't be here, but my daughters and granddaughters probably will be. How will their lives be?

The humanitarian organization Oxfam has predicted the world will run out of food around 2050 when a growing world population exceeds food growing capacity. Of course, that will be horrific for people in third-world countries. Those here in the United States will probably still be able to eat, just not all the things we know.

"Think of the bright side," they say, and here it is: some crops will get a boost from climate change. Getting more atmospheric carbon dioxide has doubled the potency of poppies, the plant used to make heroin. Cocaine will also do well because the coca bush is one that's likely to adapt to the changes. "Coca is kind of unique, because it's got a very heavy wax cuticle, a layer on the leaves," said Charles Helling, a chemist at US Department of Agriculture, "so that tends to protect it from water loss." We wonder, *Will the Generation X or Millennials come up with ways to keep food from going extinct, or will they all be high as kites watching the seeming end of the world?* And what shall I do now? Go to protests, write letters to my Congressperson, or what? As children of the 1940s, this was not on our radar, tragically. How do we make peace with this seemingly bleak future?

While we Boomers caught a time of milk and honey, it's hard to face what our descendants will meet.

Born Lucky

JACK WILLIAMSON

In the 2017 film "*Lucky*," Harry Dean Stanton plays a ninety-year-old atheist who has outlived and out-smoked his contemporaries as he comes to terms with his own mortality. I was captivated by Harry. He moved me to realize I too am an aging lucky guy. (Harry died in 2017 at the age of ninety-one.)

But in contrast, I also know there are many people who seem to be born unlucky. I am reminded of this hard reality almost every time I watch the evening news. I also come face-to-face with those who less fortunate than I weekly as I deliver "Meals on Wheels," interacting with an average of fifteen unlucky folks in dire straits.

While I've certainly had my ups and downs in life and a fair share of failures and setbacks, I have also had more than my fair share of good luck. Some folks tell me I'm blessed, and maybe that's the better word, but as I see it, it's not because some deity chooses to "bless" me instead of others, but rather because I see myself as simply lucky.

Here are just ten of the many ways I count myself lucky:

1. Lucky to be born in a country of freedom. I could easily have been born in many other places offering far less opportunities to be lucky.

2. Lucky to have good and loyal friends, which enables us to provide mutual support, understanding, and acceptance.

3. Lucky to have been born to parents who loved me even though I was considered the "black sheep," maybe because I have always marched to a different drummer. To this day, I hear a different beat than every other member of my family.

4. Lucky, as a progressive liberal, to have had successful careers within two conservative institutions—an evangelical church denomination and the military.

5. Lucky to still be able to volunteer, serving others rather than needing volunteers to support and help me.

6. Lucky to have good health at this stage of my life.

7. Lucky to be financially comfortable in my retirement years.

8. Lucky that curiosity remains a core of who I am. I still enjoy exploring new thoughts, learning new skills, and integrating new life lessons.

9. Lucky to have healthy children and grandchildren who love me and are each helping to make this world a better place.

10. Lucky to be married to a hospice nurse. Who knows if or when I'll need his skilled and loving care, but I consider him a wonderful partner and a cherished medical backstop.

I am increasingly aware of how lucky I've been throughout so many transitions in my life. While I am wildly grateful for my lucky (privileged) life, I am seeking more reasons to be grateful for that privilege.

I was startled this morning to receive news that a former neighbor's privilege of life ended last night. He died suddenly in his sleep. Mike and I were the same age, more than seventy-six years old, both older than the 75.1 years life expectancy for American males. If I depart this planet like Mike, it will be the icing on the cake of my being born lucky.

Mirror, Mirror

LAURIE LEINONEN

I remember my father finding me singing "*Oh, You Beautiful Doll!*" while gazing into a mirror when I was about seven years old. I had learned the song on the piano. I can still picture the hallway mirror that I stood in front of, swaying back and forth as I sang. I was totally enthralled with my performance and remember him happening upon me but not interrupting me. He used to call me "Dollee Babee," so it might not be too much to say I probably thought I was pretty cute. I prefer to call it innocent vanity.

Nowadays, mirrors and window reflections are not quite so enthralling. I have an inner mirror image that I prefer not to distort with reality. I have read somewhere that we do not see ourselves as others see us or even as reflected in a mirror. Therefore, I am going with my inner delusional imagery. As they say, in our mind's eye, we are always young and in prime physical shape, even when in our nineties. The reflection looking back at me is sometimes my mother's or my father's or it can suddenly startle me with an entirely unrecognizable person.

In the 1990's, when my daughter was in college, we went to the Metropolitan Museum in New York City. I was recently divorced and visited her as often as I could. I remember standing in line together when she suddenly stepped out. When she came back, ducking under the cordoned line with a big grin, I honestly didn't recognize her. She looked totally foreign to me. It was such a strange sensation. I think it may have been some odd combination of the perceived and explicit imageries of both myself and my daughter colliding.

I have had similar experiences waiting to meet a family member whom I have not seen for some time. I find myself focusing so hard that I will mistake someone else for them and then feel foolish when I am wrong. Once, while passing by a Starbucks on my way to baggage claim, I noticed a young woman, animatedly, holding a cell phone in front of her face. My eyes were drawn to her colorful skirt and tousled hair. When my daughter met me, it turned out that she was filming me as I strolled by.

Another time, while heading to my departure gate, I decided to stop for a snack at Dunkin' Donuts. As I walked to the end of the line, out of the corner of my eye, I glimpsed a handsome young man, standing quite relaxed with arms folded and a lovely smile. I almost passed by when I suddenly realized it was my son-in-law with my grandson in a stroller. I couldn't believe it! We were traveling to Seattle from different destinations for a family reunion, and while I knew we might be passing through the airport at about the same time, I really didn't expect to run into them.

How do we recognize ourselves and those we are close to when we hold these memories of bodies that don't change in the same way they do outside our minds? Which is more real? What do we see in the mirror? With our eyes? In our memories? As expectations?

Roethke's World

SARAH MASSEY-WARREN

The Waking

I wake to sleep and take my waking slow.
I feel my fate in what I cannot fear.
I learn by going where I have to go.

—Thedore Roethke

"Don't worry about it until you get there," says Morgan, my younger daughter, as we walk, masked, for hours. I tell her I find going back to the university in the fall untenable, given that the administration expects us to teach multiple scenarios within each class to meet student needs. Multiply that by four classes, three different subjects, eighty students, and paltry pay. We have to give the department feedback in less than twenty-four hours. "Just write what you feel," she says, and I do. I learn by going where I have to go.

We think by feeling. What is there to know?
I hear my being dance from ear to ear.
I wake to sleep, and take my waking slow.

—Theodore Roethke

It's spring. After being cooped up in solitude for six weeks, except for long walks, I watch the crocus, then daffodils, then tulips vibrate. They gyrate with the grass. My being dances blade to blade, bulb to bulb, seed to seed. It's garden season, but three feet of snow pummel the tulips. They rebound and take their waking slow.

> Of those so close beside me, which are you?
> God bless the Ground! I shall walk softly there,
> And learn by going where I have to go.
>
> —Theodore Roethe

Theodore Roethke came from a family of greenhouse builders. Born in Saginaw, Michigan, he suffered from abandonment, depression, mood swings, and wild creative urges. He struggled between the demands of art, the demands of teaching at Michigan State University, the impossibility of finding the time to do it all. He fit no mold, once weighed 225 pounds, trusted nobody. At first, critics scoffed. Then they listened. He won the Pulitzer. I will never win the Pulitzer. Roethke inspires me, another Michigan native, with his visceral, spiritual tie to the land. All you can do is bless the ground and walk softly, safely there. I ache to live in a greenhouse and designed greenhouses for indoor/outdoor unity in Landscape Architecture.

> Light takes the Tree; but who can tell us how?
> The lowly worm climbs up a winding stair;
> I wake to sleep, and take my waking slow.
>
> —Theodore Roethke

Roethke groped for a spiritual center. He hailed the lowly worm. My spade turned soil to plant Alpine Aster. A worm crawled up; my Rottie-Beagle mix, Roethke, watched. Morgan gave him to me to make sure I didn't adopt another full-blown Rottweiler, as they tend to pull me over. The Humane Society said he was five, although he was at least seven and didn't resemble Boulder purebred designer dogs. His heart filled 90 percent of his body. Roethke took his waking slow. I still ask the dog-forsaken couch if it wants to go for a walk.

> Great Nature has another thing to do
> To you and me; so take the lively air,
> And, lovely, learn by going where to go.
>
> –Theodore Roethke

Great Nature shakes us into creativity—whether art, design, writing, gardening, love—by the demands of growth. Walk, take the lively air—it's all that will get us through this damn pandemic. If we listen to the White House, we won't survive. We must learn to grow. Where do the students come in? Or the univeristy's lust for profit? Mom, worry about it when you get there. Learn by going where to go.

> This shaking keeps me steady. I should know.
> What falls away is always. And is near.
> I wake to sleep, and take my waking slow.
> I learn by going where I have to go.
>
> –"The Waking" by Theodore Roethke

Roethke, the dog, collapsed from heart cancer in January—it filled 90 percent of his body. The vets guessed that he was at least twelve. I never knew dogs could get heart cancer. Roethke, the poet, died at age fifty-five of a heart attack while swimming. What falls away is always, and is near. This shaking keeps me alert, I should know and learn by going where I have to go.

Pandemic Garden

LAURA K. DEAL

Going outside was the last thing I wanted to do. The smoky air baked in ninety-seven-degree late-summer heat and carried the scent of distant wildfires. But six months earlier, back in March of 2020, when the world shut down and the promise of spring was in the air, my instinct was to plant seeds. I had started by planting tomatoes, beans, kale, lettuce, basil, Romanesque broccoli, and turban squash. In those first uncertain weeks of the lockdown, I loved finding tiny new sprouts pushing their way up through the soil. In April and May, my spouse and I dug the garden beds, pulling out grass, harebell, and catnip by the roots. I carried my seedlings outside during the day and back in at night, until the soil and sky warmed enough to put them in the garden. When my husband brought sprouting potatoes up from the cold storage in the basement, I planted those as well.

All summer, I watered and weeded, murmuring encouragement to the plants. The Romanesque broccoli that I thought had died returned with vigor, and the squash, after spending weeks with two small leaves, suddenly sent out vines that eventually grew to become fifteen feet tall, with leaves larger than dinner plates. In July, the tomato harvest began, the Tiger's Eye Beans had dried enough to pick, and volunteer amaranth took over one of the beds. The cold frame contained a tangled jungle of kale, bolted lettuce, basil, oregano, and even a volunteer tomato that must have been planted by some small critter having a snack.

The long weeks of temperatures over ninety degrees that summer stressed us all. Leaves turned brown and fell, despite my daily pilgrimage to bring water to thirsty roots. Something broke leaves and fruit off tomato vines, leaving only naked stalks sticking out like a Tinker Toy creation. Later, I discovered the culprits were tomato hornworms, eating my plants now so that later they could pollinate my sage as hummingbird moths. The tomatoes still bore fruit, the three squashes would soon be ready for harvest, and underground, the potatoes had grown large.

Standing there in the summer heat, I reached back, in memory, to the spring, when the garden was my refuge and the site of my hope, and planting was a tangible thing I could do in a world that seemed then so profoundly uncertain. As I had planted, I looked forward to the days when the harvest would come in and my hopes would be fulfilled, if we survived the pandemic until then.

Those late summer days, I struggled to shrug off the weight of the world in order to apply sunscreen, put on my sunhat, and tie on the mask that I had made to protect from disease, which also made it possible to breathe in the smoke-filled air. Then I stepped into the heat to visit the plants that I had tended so carefully all those months. The world seemed to be caught in a holding pattern, even as the days shortened and the promise of cooler weather made me yearn for fall. I wondered if I would ever want to host house concerts again, or mingle in a crowd, or meet a stranger face-to-face without a mask. I wondered if next summer would be like this one, still in a strange pause, even as the garden marked the passage of time.

Balance

BETH SHAW

The word "balance" brings to mind the image of a scale or a see-saw with a child, short legs dangling, perched at each end. Balance implies stability, steadiness, and even stasis, yet the slightest weight shift on either side will upset it. To regain balance on a see-saw once it has been upset, the children must readjust their body positions, and this is not a simple operation. It requires complex coordination between mind and body so that all the senses and body parts involved work together to re-establish equilibrium.

In a New Yorker article (dated January 8, 2018), Siddhartha Mukherjee, writing about his father's death, speaks of the enormous effort and incredibly complex systems required to maintain the apparent constancy of a human body functioning smoothly. He describes the frantic effort of doctors in a New Delhi clinic, where his father was taken after a fall, to re-establish balance in his body when his brain could no longer provide the coordination required to maintain equilibrium. Instruments constantly measured blood pressure, temperature, salt, and fluid levels, but, Mukherjee says, "What we didn't measure—couldn't measure—was how hard his body was working to bestill these values, how much 'unnatural vigilance was required to keep things going."

So, although balance may look effortless, it is not. Though we may hope and strive for balance in many aspects of our lives, we usually find ourselves a little off kilter here, and a bit off-center there, and the effort to keep from, as we say, "falling apart" can be exhausting.

My eighty-six-year-old husband has dementia. He doesn't have extreme memory loss, but like a two or three-year-old, he is unable to comprehend how a simple tool works—something he's used easily for decades.

This situation is hard for him but also for me and for others, especially the son who has been asked to take on responsibility for his father's rental business. My husband has always had total confidence in his abilities and intelligence, so it's hard for him to let go, but he more or less realizes he's no longer able to make rational decisions. He is literally, physically, off balance much of the time, but this is only an outward symptom of what must be happening in his psyche. The inner struggle between the instinct to maintain control and the awareness of loss and independence must be constant, terrifying, and exhausting. And for those of us close to him, the uncertainty about what he can and can't do or understand, which changes almost from day to day, is very disorienting. For caretakers and loved ones of people suffering from dementia, the struggle to find the right balance between respect, empathy, frustration, and grief can be extremely stressful.

For all of us, life is a daily balancing act. No matter how sure and steady a person may seem, behind the calm surface lie innumerable tensions—between work and play, duty and pleasure, activity and rest, and so many more. We teeter-totter on the see-saws of our lives— nerves, muscles, mind, and body struggling mightily to maintain a steady balance until one day it all ends in complete stasis.

Take Time for Your Soul

LUELLEN RAMEY

W hen you discover something that nourishes your soul and brings you joy, care enough about yourself to make room for it in your life. Nurture yourself, nurture your soul.

The *soul, spirit, or inner being*—these are words for the immaterial essence of a person that many believe precedes one's earthly existence and continues after that existence has concluded.

Our lives are dominated by busyness: work, family, errands, and entertainment. Do this, fix that, check it off the to-do list. Often we feel lazy if we aren't doing. But the loss of soul connection creates a void, an emptiness that cries for fulfillment.

In all of life, but especially during grieving, it's important to take time for the soul—to connect with the deeper inner part of life. This begins by giving ourselves permission and time to be soulful, to take seriously this aspect of ourselves. We have a need and a right to spend part of our lives caring for our souls. This is about quality of life, not output. It's about treasuring what is unique, valuable, and internal to ourselves.

Beginning my day with a simple habit that connects me with my inner being, I make my coffee and sit in my favorite chair, looking out toward the morning sun on the Flatirons or the clouds surrounding the mountains. I gaze outward during this quiet time and am in a receptive space within myself. Ideas, thoughts, and feelings surface. These moments can lead to creative ideas or simply be calm and peaceful, a gentle start to my day.

One of the strongest places I connect with my inner being is in the presence of other people who I meet at a soul level. It happens whenever a dialogue takes place in which both people are truly present, tuning into really hearing each other. To voice something you're feeling with another person who is totally present embodies soul and love.

When people in a group speak of experiences that have affected them deeply, trusting in their vulnerability, we are meeting at a soul level, and compassion and healing energy enter our space.

Nature connects me with my spirit. A beautiful hike last evening amid the spring green foothills and newly budded trees and the purple, yellow, and white wildflowers—the smell of blossoms and pine—renewed my spirit.

There are many ways to nourish the soul: meditation, prayer, inspirational reading, journaling, art, music, communing with nature, time with your beloved companion animal, quietness—any source of beauty or creativity. What particular experiences will nourish your soul? No one can prescribe that for you; it is something you must determine for yourself. You will know by the feeling of enjoyment or peace that it brings you. Experiment. Especially notice what totally absorbs you. Treasure yourself.

Transitions

SUSAN JOSEPHS

After a delayed flight from Denver, I walked into my son and daughter-in-love's (my daughter's sweeter term for "in-law") Los Angeles kitchen. I carefully washed my hands before Alex handed me my two-week-old granddaughter, Louise Belle (Lulu). Alex sighed with new mother exhaustion, relieved to have my helping hands. I sighed with grandmother elation, delighted to be needed. My heart melted as I held my son's first child and felt this little love bundle's baby softness and sweetness.

How different it feels to hold my granddaughter than it did to hold my daughter and son. I recognize their new-parent awe, frustration, fatigue, and concern that somehow they're not doing something right. When a friend and her husband brought home their first child, the husband lamented, "When do the real parents show up?" Babies don't arrive with instruction manuals.

I relished holding Lulu after she had nursed. She snuggled close, dreaming away, as all eight pounds of her slept in my arms. My son had also loved being held while he napped. But now, I had nothing else to do. How different this was from holding my children, when a million chores awaited attention.

Carefully trying to weave my role as mother-in-law, I gladly folded laundry, shopped for food, prepared meals, and attempted to give these new parents some space. During my visit, I relished Lulu's daily growing curiosity. Her entire life is ahead of her as my son and his wife enter this expansive new chapter. What a joy it is to watch my son embrace fatherhood.

I've waited a long time for grandchildren. My son is forty-two. My daughter had her son at forty-one. And, at seventy-seven, I am also *losing* friends and family. The husband of one of my dearest friends recently died at the age of ninety. I attended Evans' memorial service just days after meeting my granddaughter. The juxtaposition of new life and death has never felt more vivid.

Family members emotionally eulogized Evans with tales of his pervasive influence on their lives. Friends from his Peace Corps days reminded us of the *many* stages of life we all go through and how even our smallest actions deeply affect people. The collective love and caring among those who gathered to share and remember Evans' life was palpable. This loving memorial was no less awe-inspiring than holding my new grandchild. Our time on earth is finite. My elder awareness made both experiences more precious.

Gazing at my granddaughter, I kept wondering how her consciousness will evolve; how will she express the nurture and nature she will inhabit? Evans had utilized his nature and nurture, creating an expansive life, traveling widely, and leaving a legacy of lasting memories and relationships. Becoming a grandmother at this later stage of life gives me a wider window on the world. I am so grateful for all of life's stages and mysteries.

How Courage Looks As I Age

MARY ANN PALIANI

A ging is a process that starts at birth and ends with death. It's not just the domain of the over sixty-five crowd. What role does courage play in our lives as we grow older? Throughout our time in this world, we encounter a wide spectrum of experiences that frighten us or that require us to endure pain, grief, or loss. How do we deal with these challenges? Do we courageously face them head-on, effectively using lessons learned from previous experiences, or do we collapse under their weight? Do we deliberately test ourselves with new challenges—physical, intellectual, or emotional undertakings that force us to come to grips with some of our deepest fears and to grow—or do we play it safe and walk away? I maintain that as we move towards our final destiny, courage helps us manage and enrich our lives, and the lives of those around us.

At the age of eighty-three, I'm kind of lucky. I don't have immediate family, health issues, or financial concerns. Most of my friends are decades younger than I. So, I am spared many of the things that confront other people of my vintage. But, what is key in my life is an insatiable desire to discover the world and myself—my physical, emotional, and intellectual limits. To satisfy the urge, I deliberately court unfamiliar experiences. You might say I'm a challenge junky. But taking on a new experience inevitably evokes fear! When I face one of these "tests," I fill the unknown with my own story—one that underscores all the risks and dangers imaginable. Courage then forces me to face those real, or more often imagined, concerns up close and intimately. If I succeed, I look for something more daunting. If I fail, I go back and try again.

I've been training for a challenging hike in Patagonia—the Torres del Paine trek. Over the past several months, I've been working with a mountain guide to prepare for the venture. On one of our training outings, I had to cross a stream on a board that was six or seven inches wide. At my age, balance is not one of my strengths. Initially, I crossed the stream hanging onto the guide for dear life; I was scared. Where was Yoda, the Jedi master from Star Wars, when I needed him? Then, with some trepidation, I repeated the exercise using just my walking sticks for balance. Finally, I crossed the stream without assistance from either the guide or the sticks. But the capstone of the exercise was walking *backwards* on the board over the stream, unassisted. Each one of these mini challenges demanded courage. But, in the end, I tested my limits, vanquished my fears, and further added to my portfolio of self-knowledge and personal growth. More importantly, I showed some of my juniors that age does not limit what's possible.

The essence of courage is the conscious and deliberate choice to engage a challenge. Pursuing challenges throughout one's entire life influences not only the quality of an individual's life, but also transmits important core values to present and future generations. Ultimately, it enriches the fabric of our evolving society.

What Grows

SARAH MASSEY-WARREN

We wake, if we ever wake at all, to my mystery, beauty, violence. "Seems like we're just set down here," a woman said to me recently, "and don't nobody know why."

—Annie Dillard, *Pilgrim at Tinker Creek*

The veggies and perennials impatiently strain at their containers. Balled-up roots wrap their soil. I finger the strands and set them into the newly prepped beds. A month ago, I seeded multi-colored salad greens, spinach, carrots, and poppy seeds into separate beds. The poppies, a gift from my master gardener Wisconsin sister, Becky, never appeared, although the veggies poke colorfully from their brown beds. The twenty-six inches of snow and single-digit April temperatures didn't help.

Dirt crawls under my fingernails like memory. I smell worms and cigarette smoke—the presence of Max, my nephew, Becky's first son. An addicted smoker, he passed a cigarette to me as we stood on the driveway in deep snow after another full family Christmas in 2014. As the outsiders ("you share the dark side," Becky said), we huddled jacketless against the dark silence of Omaha cold, snow wet on our faces, stomping our shoes.

I don't smoke.

Even now, Max appears on my couch, the cat between us, passing a cigarette. He watches the planting.

Pushing the perennials deep into the dark, wet earth, I miss Max, who died in October 2016 of anorexia (the family curse) and marijuana laced with fentanyl. Usually, Max grew his own weed in a basement in Madison. His younger brother, Peter, died at the age of thirteen weeks in 1992, so Becky is childless. She always wanted a family. I never did. Max and my daughters lined up closely in age, following each other into the world within a three-year time span. My two daughters thrive; from them, I cultivate shimmering joy and shattering pain.

Thunderhead Stonecrop. Catchfly Silene. Blue Campanella. Lavender. The new plants snuggle next to the Ninebark, sedums, and other perennials from last summer. Will they all get along? Plants and trees thrive on diversity; monocultures fail. Humans could learn something from that. "Humans are overcomplicated houseplants," observes Anika Gorham. Frankly, I don't think we've evolved that far.

The excited shrieks from the toddler next door assail the plants. I think of my students, who constantly tell me "what the older generation thinks." "The older generation doesn't care about the environment and climate change like we do," my environmental writing students ironically assure me. Wait until the toddler addresses them as "the older generation."

Which generation is Max now? He always grouched about the power of "The Man," and refused to work. A gifted artist and talented musician, he never wrapped his head around reality, losing himself in drugs and a hermit's existence. His was the soft soul of yearning and rootlessness.

Financially secure retired teachers before Scott Walker smashed the unions, Becky and her husband work part-time in a greenhouse and travel to exotic places. Becky owns a gardening business. I'm so jealous, I can hardly breathe. Becky would give her eye teeth for a son as lucky as my daughters. We both find solace in plants. Why does anything or anyone grow?

"The most beautiful thing we can experience is the mysterious," writes Einstein. "It is the source of all true art and science." I urge another plant into the garden, awaiting the beauty, mystery, or violence.

Wading

MARINA FLORIAN

I dove under a thunderous wave and laughed out loud. As the set relentlessly continued to crash in at high tide, I dove again and again, laughing at the sheer joy of dodging the waves' potent force. Later, as I walked down the wide beach, I found myself smiling broadly as I watched local Costa Rican children kicking balls on the beach, playing in the sand and water. Arriving back in Boulder, I gave my hairdresser free rein and left an inch and a half of my tresses on the salon floor. After wading through the unruly, unflinchingly unpredictable waters of the pandemic, it was time to move on. I was elated.

Yet, then, the question soon arose: how does one re-enter the world after fourteen months of living a limited lifestyle forced on us by the threat of a possibly fatal disease? As the weight of the pandemic lifts, how do we restructure our lives?

As I begin to flex my social muscles again, I realize that they have grown rusty. I have found myself overwhelmed by having dinner with six people, thinking, *"How does one interact with SO many people in the room?"*

It has been challenging to make plans with friends. While on our own during the pandemic, each of us developed new routines that enabled us to maintain our sanity. Many of us have grown set in our ways. Now, in engaging with others, we may have to modify our new rhythms. I know that I have become less flexible and am actively assessing alterations to my routine. Yet I find that it is imperative to incorporate these changes slowly. I need time to absorb the changes and gradually open my closeted world.

Here are a few things I have noticed during this transition:

- I used to have dinner with friends around 7:00 p.m, but now many of my friends prefer 6:00 p.m. We are attempting to compromise on the exact time. And a close friend of mine recently fell asleep during a dinner. Her timeclock has not been reset.

- I am sleeping peacefully now. During the pandemic, I always woke up in the middle of the night feeling unsettled. The "fight or flight" instinct interrupted my sleep patterns.

- Going out without wearing a mask is a bit awkward but freeing. Almost everyone I pass during my afternoon walk smiles broadly at me, and I return that smile.

- I now listen captively to "American Dirt" and other Audible selections, music, or the neighborhood birds when I am walking. During COVID, instead, I constantly called friends, as it was one of the only ways to connect. Now, this need is satisfied during daily life as we can interact in person.

- Everyone is unique. We all need to process this transition and make changes as we see fit.

I feel privileged to take part in this process. We are extremely lucky to live in a country where we have access to vaccines. And now, as the tide is changing course, I am wading cautiously back into the water.

Looking Back, Lucky Me

JANAT HOROWITZ

I can't tell you why, but luck has always been with me. As a ten-year-old, I would ride the trolley to downtown Pittsburgh to walk around the stores. One day a man asked me if I liked birds, and I said yes. He invited me to his home; I went—gasp!—and he gave me a cage with a parakeet. I took my prize home on the trolley.

Flash forward: after moving to Colorado in 1978, I worked at Aspen City Hall and was placed in an office with no windows; here I was surrounded by beauty without being able to see any of it. Hitchhiking home, I complained to the driver, "I wish I had a job outside, such as being a rafting guide." He replied, "My best friend owns a rafting company; want his number?" I was hired and ran the rivers for three summers.

After my divorce in 1986, the Gods of Fortune struck again. I had paid for a month to be at the famed Esalen Institute in Big Sur, California, and soon they hired me for five years. During that time, my red Pontiac Grand Prix died, and because I was broke, I put a sign on the bulletin board that I wanted a free working car. A community member gave me his yellow station wagon for free, and I used that car for years.

Later, in Santa Cruz, I was hired as a barista. The pay was dismal, but the owner said that she had a place above her garage where I could live for free. Soon, I was part of a therapy group, and to my surprise, two of the people in the group were multi-millionaires. The cafe owner decided to sell, and I mentioned it to the group. This couple then offered to loan me a $50,000 as a down payment for the café, and I became the owner.

Later, I wanted a dog. A friend suggested a Tibetan Terrier, and they are fairly rare. I had a dream telling me to go to the Humane Society. I went, and there in a cage was a Tibetan Terrier. Magoo was my companion for eleven years.

In 2004, I ended up in a dark basement apartment in Denver when a friend came to visit. He said he was looking for an assistant at an art center and wanted me. Then, I had a great job living on a beautiful mountaintop art center surrounded by 450 acres.

Five years later, there was the recession, and I was laid off and lost my paradise. Where to go? What to do? There was a message on my phone from an old boyfriend wanting me to move to Monterey to work for him, with the possibility of rekindling our romance. We're married and have been together for thirteen years at the time of this writing.

Why have I been so very lucky? I think positively and believe life will support me. May we all be so fortunate!

Glioblastoma

PEGGY WALLIS

A glioblastoma is a malignant tumor affecting the brain or spine. Treatment can help, but this condition can't be cured. Despite improved surgical techniques, therapies, and radiotherapies, the prognosis for this type of pathology remains very poor, and most patients die within twelve to eighteen months from diagnosis. My husband is a neurosurgeon, so I know about these things.

The reason that a glioblastoma is so deadly is that it cannot be completely removed. Even when it looks like you have excised the entire tumor, a cell or two will remain, waiting to send tentacles out into the surrounding brain tissue and take over. I've heard that with all the surgical improvements and neuropharmacological advances that have taken place over the past five years, the survival rate for a patient with a glioblastoma has increased by five months. My husband thinks that outcome is remarkable, better than expected, but it looks like agonizingly slow progress to me.

When I was in college, I took a course in logic and learned about Achilles paradox, an argument attributed to the fifth-century Greek philosopher Zeno and one of his four paradoxes described by Aristotle in the treatise *Physics*. The paradox concerns a race between the fleet footed Achilles and a slow-moving tortoise. The paradox is this: if the tortoise has a head start, however small, Achilles will never catch up. For a while, he is covering the gap between himself and the tortoise; a new gap is created. No matter how quickly Achilles closes each gap, the tortoise will always open a new, smaller one, and remain just ahead. Even if the gap becomes miniscule, it is still finite. It still exists. Arguments like this make me want to cry and never take another course in logic. I just knew Achilles could beat that tortoise.

So what does the Achilles paradox have to do with a glioblastoma? I believe that there is a link between the two, between removing a glioblastoma and the Achilles paradox, for in both cases you are so close to a conclusion and yet so far away. That one cancer cell that hides within healthy tissue is the plodding tortoise that can never be overtaken. It's "almost but not quite" every time.

Having followed the news these past weeks, the demonstrations and calls for action after the murder of George Floyd, and the cries that Black Lives Matter, I cannot help but see this country's legacy of racism and white supremacy as a glioblastoma that has never been fully excised. That last cell, ready to invade the healthy tissue with its poison, is always there, hiding in plain sight and poised to take over. And like Achilles, no matter how close we get to our better selves, that small but finite gap has never been bridged. We fool ourselves into thinking that the cancer is gone, and that we are inclusive, but cancer is tricky. Racism is ingrained. And the tortoise plods on. Yet, I still believe that Achilles can catch up with the tortoise and that we will, someday, remove that last malignant cell. If we are honest about our intentions and relentless in our efforts, it could happen.

Connections

RICHARD MANSBACH

A circle of chairs. Stone fireplace at one end and a kitchen at the other, its sliding silver panels along the serving line closed but unable to keep the food prep noises contained. Tables on the sides containing markers, name tags, sign-up sheets, mugs, masks, water bottles, plastic cups, drums, and jackets. Wide windows looking out at evergreens and high desert brush.

Thirty-plus men were greeting each other with hugs and slaps on the back, grabbing a coffee, or filling water bottles from one of two blue barrel containers as we were called to circle up.

I recognized two-thirds of the men from previous weekends. I am part of a national organization that puts on rites of passage weekends for teenage boys. I founded this center in 2008 in Prescott, Arizona. I had been "called" for the work of mentoring teenage boys through my own rites of passage experience and had flown in the day before to staff, this time as an elder as opposed to a leader.

It had been a year, and I didn't realize how thirsty I was to be in this environment, for after being introduced and asked to say a few words, I was overcome with emotion, like a gasp for air. It only lasted a few seconds, but behind my scrunched-up eyes was so much gratitude.

For the men who had been with me from the beginning, for the men who kept showing up, for the lives transformed, and for the second generation of leaders that were mentored by the generation I mentored.

Asked how I got the center established from scratch, I said, "Coffee." The creation story involved me talking to men over coffee and sharing stories from other centers I had staffed. The founding question became, "Were you enrolled by Richard, tearing up over coffee?"

I was one of the "grandfathers" on this weekend, a role honored multiple times. Certainly, for our age and the decades of experience on the planet, also for the unfiltered love a grandfather gives to his grandchildren. In practice, sitting on a white plastic chair in forty-degree weather as an initiate sits opposite—some nervous, unsure, and unable to look me in the eye, others more present and confident. My intention is to speak to the light within them, to let them know I was there to support their gift being revealed in support of our tribe.

The richness comes from working with the boys, facilitating one-on-one or coaching them in processes. Intuition tells a man working with a fourteen-year-old who lives in a foster home, abandoned by his parents and relatives, that he might want a hug. He asks the boy. Hesitant at first, the boy then glomps on and doesn't let go for five minutes.

By the end of the weekend, my soul was replenished and overflowing with love. Asked to bless the newly initiated boys who were now considered Journeymen (on their way to manhood), I stood and once again was immediately overcome with emotion. Seconds later, I was thanking them for the privilege and honor of supporting their journey.

Exploring Caves

JACK WILLIAMSON

Not all those who wander are lost.

—J.R.R. Tolkien

I have wandered into few restricted caves. I have also explored more open spaces, skied down Austrian mountains, swam in powerful oceans and picturesque lakes, seen masterpieces of art in spectacular museums, and, best of all, flown to countries to live and absorb cultures different from my homeland. In retrospect, I loved them all!

Pico Iyer says it well:

> If travel is like love, it is, in the end, mostly because its a heightened state of awareness, in which we are mindful, receptive, undimmed by familiarity and ready to be transformed. That is why the best trips, like the best love affairs, never really end.

I can't say cave exploration of the personal and interior type has been a love affair for me. Those caves have been fear-laden, triggering visits to my inner dark spaces—recesses of my shadow side. It is only after tunneling through strata of familial and cultural expectations that self-compassion and healthy self-love emerged. The framing that James Hollis, the renowned Jungian therapist, offers rings true for me: " … to seize permission to be who I really am—to energize and inspire myself on my journey to create a life of personal authority, integrity, and fulfillment."

Several years ago, the world was transfixed by pictures of the treacherous confines of a flooded Thai cave, where twelve boys and their soccer coach were trapped deep within the cave's labyrinth. Not only did the care and concern for the team's wellbeing span nations and time zones, but the actual heart-throbbing rescue did as well, with over half the expert diving team coming from across the world.

During my college years, I explored Kentucky's Mammoth Cave, feeling my way into its inner, foreboding recesses—a haunting sense of being pulled into its eerie dark. This cave is a long system of chambers and subterranean passageway; its ceilings are covered in nineteenth-century visitors' signatures.

Only in recent years have I found the courage to face the shadows in my own caves, hidden within my typically bright, public persona. Little did I know then that the memories of those dark scenes would serve as a personal metaphor, like the shafts of a miner's light revealing my interior queries.

Sometimes, I can still feel lost and fearful of drowning while trying to find an exit from the frightful dark. What sometimes feels like the brink of deep loss, mysterious synapses link to my inner explorer's compass and once again point the way to my true north, allowing light to break through, welcoming life-rescuing insight.

Similar to the young Thai soccer players, with the help of friends, I am escorted and tethered back into the welcomed sunshine of familiar open places and spaces where personal authority, integrity, and fulfillment now reside.

Yes, occasionally I wander into caves, but I am not lost.

The Limits of Science

LAURA DEAL

The search for meaning is not limited to science: it is constant
and continuous—all of us engage in it during all our waking
hours [and] the search continues even in our dreams.

—Ervin László.

Recently, I went to a party for my husband's coworkers and their families. Most of the people there were scientists, fully grounded in a reality that can be measured, studied, and (at least sometimes) proven. One woman asked about my current work, which involves studying a historical character so deeply that I will, eventually, be able to present a program as that character. The focus of my study is the Jungian analyst Marion Woodman, who had several profound experiences in her life that modern science has no framework to explain. As I told one of Marion's stories, the scientist raised her eyebrows higher and reframed the story in words that utterly dismissed its deeper meaning. For me, the importance of the story was not about whether the interpretation that Marion and her husband had of the cause and effect of events was scientifically provable, but rather that they consciously transformed their roles within their marriage because of their shared experience.

Still, I didn't press the point with the scientist. I've learned that it's easier not to argue.

Less than a week before that conversation, I was having a very blue day. Tears threatened for no reason that I could understand. Certainly, the state of the world evokes grief, but that is an everyday weight that I have learned to lug about and attend to only when I have some privacy and quiet. This was something more than that—immediate and urgent. I had dreamed that morning about a dear friend who had moved away. While running errands a few hours later, I saw the mother of one of my daughter's childhood friends, whom I had just learned was also planning to move away. So, my friend was on my mind. I think of her every day, but this was different.

The urge to call her grew until I couldn't ignore it. When she answered the phone and we said hello, she burst into tears. Only a few hours before, she and her husband had had their eighteen-year-old cat euthanized. I understood then why my intuition to call her had been so strong and why my own mood had been so down all day.

I've spent my life trying to explain my experiences to people who only understand things they can explain in scientific terms. It's become quite clear that the multitude of synchronicities I notice would mean nothing to them. Perhaps they find comfort in keeping their worldview narrow, but I find comfort in seeing meaning in the things that science can't explain. This wasn't the first time that my friend's mood affected mine from a distance before I understood why. It wasn't the first time that I have listened to my intuition and then discovered why my mind was urging me to take action. It wasn't the first time that my "radar" was attuned to someone a thousand miles away.

I appreciate that some scientists remain open to the mystery of things that science can't yet explain, and I'm grateful for scientists who help us understand and develop solutions to thorny problems. I trust the scientists who promised that the COVID-19 vaccine provided more protection than risk. I certainly believe that there is an important role for scientific inquiry in this grand human experiment. But I also know, in a way I can't prove to anyone, that there are more things in this heaven and earth than is dreamt of in the skeptic's philosophy.

Finality

BETH SHAW

For about five years, I've belonged to a support group for caregivers of ill or disabled spouses. Until recently, only one regular member's spouse had died. That death happened several years ago, and at the time, I felt sympathy for the person who suffered the loss, but I didn't feel I knew him well and wasn't deeply affected.

About a week ago, I learned that the spouse of another group member had died. This time, the news jarred me to the core, as though I'd heard of the death of someone I loved and knew well, though I'd never met her. D, this woman's husband, joined the group shortly before or after I did. We've traveled more or less the same course over the years, caring for our spouses at home for quite a while, then moving them to care facilities and dealing with the practical and emotional issues this entails.

I've known D only in the support group setting, but over the past five years, I've developed a narrow but deep connection with him, as I have with several of the other group members. We've shared our vulnerabilities, our pain, our frustrations, and our feelings of guilt and love. D, in particular, has impressed and humbled me with the unwavering devotion to his wife he demonstrated, spending hour after hour holding and comforting her up to the end.

This death has been wrenching for D, but on the other hand, it's something he's been anticipating and even praying for recently, given the helpless and hopeless stage his wife had reached. One can see in his face one moment the uplift of relief and, in the next, the searing agony of loss. He's been wanting to move on, but right now, the way is unclear and the road ahead is lonely.

This event has brought me closer than anything before to contemplation of my own spouse's approaching death. It may come soon or not so soon, but he's at the stage where it would be a blessing for everyone—especially for him. He's anxious and disoriented, almost unable to communicate, helpless, dependent on others for every need. A huge burden will be lifted from my shoulders with his passing, and a huge hole has been created in my life and heart. He's still the central figure in my memories and dreams—my intrepid traveling companion, the patriarch of our large extended family. I already miss talking with him about politics, the family, all the places we've lived, and the people we've known. I even miss sharing the results of golf and tennis matches, baseball, and football games with him—things I wasn't much interested in before we met. All of this is already gone from our lives, and to some extent I've moved on, but I know that when the end comes, the shock will be intense. I see how it will be when I see D smiling and recounting a fond memory with tears in his eyes and voice.

I've wondered if the slow death of someone one loves is less painful at the end than a sudden one, but this week, I think I've learned that that's probably not the case. There are many kinds of loss, but this final one is—no matter what led up to it nor how long it took—final.

A Little Bird Told Me . . .

LAURIE LEINONEN

A campanile chimes at the half hour as commuters and tourists hustle by, some with bikes, some with roller suitcases, backpacks, cameras, or briefcases, and one young man with a "wheel" that he will no doubt zip around San Francisco on—upright—to wherever he may be going. It was his own moving sidewalk. A nifty balancing act, especially on crowded city sidewalks, but an efficient and easy commuting device.

The ferry idles at the dock while a new load of passengers boards, heading to Larkspur or Sausalito across the bay. Another ferry arrives in the neighboring slip while a gentleman settles onto the bench next to me, noshing on his aromatic "everything" bagel, drinking his coffee while soaking up the early morning sun and dockside activity. The area bustles with both folks boarding the ferry and those who've just arrived, hurrying into the restaurants for a quick bite or walking rapidly on through the ferry terminal as they head to their destinations. A ferry pilot separates the gangplank and releases the landlines of the newly reloaded ferry before backing out into the channel for its continuous back and forth journey across the picturesque bay, offering panoramic views of the city as well as photo ops of the bridges and islands it passes as it churns its way along.

There is a cacophony of chattering and clattering on the esplanade where I sit. Human sounds as well as those of birds of various shapes and sizes flocking to the railings, waddling, and pecking their way along the concrete walkway, seeking any food scraps that might have fallen or been left behind. They chatter and squawk when they spy something to nibble, if they deign to share. Quickly swooping in and landing wherever a morsel may be spotted, cocking their heads and shifting their beady little eyes rapidly back and forth, hoping to spy or peck a tasty nugget. They continually whistle and chirp at one another, somewhat optimistically and comradely, and sometimes aggressively. "Go!! Git away!" shouts one woman, waving her hands as a pigeon gets closer to her than she's comfortable with. That merely results in even more hearty scolding squawks, wing flapping, neck stretches, head swivels, and claw-footed dancing, not willing to forego the prospect of a crumb or two appearing.

One sweet, tiny black and white-chested bird lands on the railing directly in front of me. It tilts its head back and forth, blinking its eyes, and seems to warble conversationally to me. I can see its delicate throat feathers quiver as it chatters away. I cock my head and make eye contact in response, curious as to its message. It's in no rush to fly away. We share several minutes together, eye to eye, before it does flit off . . . no doubt in search of nibbles instead of conversation. I gather my things and move off through the terminal to the subway to reunite with classmates from over fifty years ago.

The Incredible Edible Car

LUELLEN RAMEY

My significant other, Marc, was ready for a new car. He researched and decided he wanted to buy the 2019 Rav4 hybrid. Production was behind schedule, so he actually had to wait till June to get just the car he wanted, with the features he wanted along with the deep ruby-red color. He immediately wanted to take a road trip in his new car. We mapped out a two-week trip: first to Chicago to visit his son, Jordan, then my cousin, Bev. Then on to a lovely place on the water in Door County, Wisconsin, on Lake Michigan. Then to Minneapolis to visit our friend, Suzanne. Then across the plains to Mt. Rushmore, Crazy Horse, and Hot Springs, then back to Boulder, Colorado.

On Saturday, after the Fourth of July, we got into his new car (with only 600 miles on it) and immediately got malfunction warning lights. We went directly to Boulder Toyota, where they said they'd have a mechanic look at the car immediately. In no time at all we were called to look under the hood. What we saw was a gnawed mess of insulation around exposed wires. The mechanic said, "Rodent damage!"

What?! We'd never heard of that, but Boulder Toyota was sure without a doubt that rodents had caused the damage. Marc filed a claim with his insurance company. They also were familiar with rodents causing damage to cars.

As we researched, we found that in an effort to "go green," manufacturers have replaced petroleum-based polymers with soy in many areas of cars, including electrical wiring harnesses, air conditioning and heating ducts, seat cushions, trunk carpeting, and various fluid containers made from plastic. Some cars have parts made of rice husks, wood, sugars, sweet-smelling substances like vanilla, peanut oil, and straw. In short, cars have become tasty and nutritious for rodents! Not only do rodents like the soy-based insulation, but they can sharpen their teeth by gnawing on the wires.

Europe was the first to pass laws requiring cars to be as recyclable as possible. Although the US does not have these laws, manufacturers build for the world.

So what happened to Marc's car? Not a lot yet. It still sits on the lot at Boulder Toyota. Although we urged them to have the car repaired in time for our scheduled road trip, that wasn't possible. Three new wiring harnesses had to be replaced, one of which has not been available. Toyota continues to be behind schedule in manufacturing this car, and parts are being used in new cars but are not yet available for repairs. They estimate thirty-five hours will be needed to rebuild the car with these new harnesses at an estimated cost of $14,000.

We went on the road trip anyway, with my car, and had a wonderful time! Sometimes, the best laid plans of mice win over the plans of men.

Grief

PEGGY WALLIS

I 've been sitting here, toying with words—a sort of fidgeting of the brain. It's lovely to sit outside, caressed by the warm breeze, with spring finally a real possibility. Trees cast flickering shadows on the back fence, and the garden is divided into slices of sun and shadow. Bees hover around the newly blossomed purple allium, dizzy with delight. But despite the warmth, the sunlight, and the pleasure of being outside, no words come.

I've never been short of words or ideas about what is true or fair. About what matters. In the abstract. But sitting in my garden, coming out of a pandemic year, I find myself at a loss for words. Until it comes back to me, the Saturday morning I drove to King Soopers for my weekly shopping. It is not my usual store, but the King Soopers on 30th Street felt strange and unfamiliar to me. I wandered around for an hour or more, looking for items that were once in a familiar place. But that's neither here nor there. On the way, I began listening to "*This American Life*," in particular a segment called "So Nice to Hear Your Voice." A young filmmaker from Portland, Oregon, had taped her weekly telephone calls with her grandmother in Assisted Living. It was riveting. For the first time, I could hear, week by week, the unraveling of a mind due to loneliness. After her facility shut down to visitors, the family, used to seeing her almost every day and taking her out, devised a plan to have someone call every day. They thought it would be for a few weeks until things returned to normal.

I sat there in the parking lot, unable to turn off the radio, listening to her voice, and describing her days. At first, she describes walking in the hall for exercise and expresses her determination to get through this. "It can't last forever," she says. In those earliest phone calls, she is happy to hear from her granddaughter and fully conversant. But as time goes by, she becomes more confused, unable to recognize a familiar voice, even with repeated prompting. Perhaps most heartbreaking is to hear her say, "I don't know what I'm doing. I think my brain has gone sideways." She passed away just before the facility opened for visitors. Death due to loneliness. I've heard they put it on death certificates, "Death to loneliness caused by COVID-19."

So to get back to ideas, which is where I started. What is true or fair, and what matters. It is true that deaths increased tremendously among the elderly population in long-term care over the course of the pandemic. It is not fair; we knew this would happen if their world was shut down, and did it anyway. It matters.

I don't know why, but I was surprised to be so profoundly touched by this story. I could almost hear the voice of my mother and all those who seemed so lost when I visited. Ghost voices, shadows of their former selves, no longer real. But it was that voice on the radio, slowly slipping away, that brought it all back and broke my heart. A character in a novel that I read recently declares, "I have to be ready for grief. You don't always see it coming." I too didn't see it coming. It surprised me, being blindsided by grief for myself and others, to hear a lost voice in the parking lot at King Soopers.

The Clock is Ticking

MARY ANN PALIANI

We have absolute certainty about only two seconds in our lives: the present moment and the moment in which we take our final breath. The interval between these two intractable limits is that diaphanous fabric, which we call time, upon which the remainder of our lives plays out. As the clock relentlessly ticks down the years, months, hours, minutes, and seconds that remain, the window of opportunity to accomplish meaningful things and complete our mission in this life gets smaller. Often, it takes a serious life crisis to remind us of our mortality and that our lives are of finite duration. Only then, do we give serious consideration to what we must do in the time that remains.

Is it ever too late to pursue our dreams, obligations, our life's mission? What gets in the way? Do we think we're too old? Do we mistrust our physical and cognitive capabilities? Do we have handicaps? Are we burdened with hostilities and negative attitudes that block meaningful relationships? In yielding to these self-imposed constraints, we risk realizing the fullest potential of our lives. Is that a risk worth taking?

Over the years, I have encountered many people who have faced significant challenges. Let me tell you about some of them who refused to say, "I can't." As a ski instructor at the National Sports Center for the Disabled in Winter Park, I probably saw every conceivable disability, often multiple disabilities, in the same person. But despite their afflictions, these people were on skis, challenging themselves to master, or at least experience, the sport, and not allowing their limitations and fears of skiing to get in the way.

Leaving this life in a state of bitterness is tragic. I had a relative who had, for decades, estranged himself from the rest of the family. As the only person with whom he stayed in contact, I found myself at his bedside during his final days. I decided to search for his long-lost nephew and attempt a reconciliation between the two. On the uncle's eighty-fifth birthday, I arranged for the two of them to communicate by phone. At the end, the nephew, traveling from California, was at his uncle's bedside in Florida, with both experiencing the grace of forgiveness at the eleventh hour. It's never too late.

So, how do we keep our focus on life, making sure that every second counts? First, remember that while we are alive, we have time. We have the power to use it or waste it. Live life in the moment. Live as if every second of life is a precious jewel that is part of a unique work of art. Commit to discovering the world—the people, places, things, and experiences in it. Equally important, pursue an inward journey. Discover who you are, and what you can do. Is there anything "broken" inside that must be fixed as far as attitudes and beliefs about oneself and others? Don't constrain yourself with "I can't" when considering your capabilities and fantasizing about your dreams. Seriously consider possibilities. Finally, face your biggest fears—one of which may be the fear of failure.

While aware that the clock is ticking, focus not on the end of life but on life itself.

Still Learning To Be Old

JACK WILLIAMSON

've always thought of myself as a life-long learner, but as someone recently told me, now at seventy-seven, you are a long-life learner. While my mind tells me I'm still in my forties or fifties, my body doggedly reminds me I'm old. I am glad to report that I am as happy and content at this stage in my life as I have ever been and am still curious enough to keep learning how to live well while old.

Breaking the Age Code is the recently released, ground-breaking research-based book by Yale professor, Dr. Becca Levy. She convincingly argues how our beliefs about aging determine how long and how well we live. Among other insights, it calls for recollections and reflections on how we learn to be old.

Instantly, my mind goes back to two elderly relatives, my early models of aging. Herbert Handy, my maternal grandfather, was a Quaker preacher who always wore a white shirt and tie, whether standing in the pulpit, sitting at meals, or bent over hoeing weeds in his garden. Aunt Helen was a Nazarene preacher who lived in our home after the passing of her husband, who was also a Nazarene preacher. Both were of the old sawdust camp-meeting vintage, cloaked in the strict and restrictive rules of Holiness theology. They were salt-of-the earth good people, but neither portrayed a model of old age I ever imagined myself replicating.

Rick Moody, a former AARP vice-president of academic affairs and a noted gerontologist, tells me that when people ask him about growing old, he thinks of what Arthur Brooks, the social scientist and columnist for *The Atlantic,* says. Brooks suggests thinking about our later life experiences as if investing in a 401(k) financial plan. "If you wait to start saving until you turn sixty, you're going to have a big problem." It's also true for how we imagine our "future selves." That was the title of a report on aging issued in 1976 by the National Institute on Aging. The foreword was written by its director, Dr. Robert Butler, who coined the term "ageism."

As with a 401(k) plan, the message and modeling needs to get to people early in their lives, and Becca Levy gets it just right. She writes, "The ideal is to think about messaging about aging starting at a young age. My research found that among young adults in their twenties, those who had taken in more negative age beliefs from their culture were twice as likely to have a cardiovascular event when they reached their sixtieth birthday."

Levy's book is not based on wishful thinking but on experiential and cross-cultural data over many years. Levy looks at problems we've always thought to be due to age, like hearing loss, memory deficits, even heart problems. It turns out that negative age beliefs are a factor in all these conditions. She notes that we have more control and influence over our lives, including later life, than we imagine.

So like that 401(k) plan, I'm "investing" in my current and future self, still learning how to be old as best I can. Hopefully, when my two grandchildren become my age, they'll remember their old grandfather as a favorable model.

We Are Ghosts To Them

RICHARD MANSBACH

F lying low over the water, we crossed the coast, and I could see palm trees and irregular shapes of green. Amidst applause and cheers, we land, balance our carry-on luggage as we walk down the stairs to the tarmac, and enter a concrete-floored building waiting for a slot to open at immigration. I enter a small, orange box, shoulder-width wide, looking down on the head of a man behind a counter.

"Look into the camera and don't smile."

He stamps my visa and points to the opposite door, and I burst into the baggage claim room. We wait a good hour before my son's luggage appears. My wife goes to the bathroom and returns with the news that there are no toilet seats and it costs a peso if you want a sheet of toilet paper.

Welcome to Cuba.

My daughter is graduating as a doctor in medicine from the Latin American School of Medicine in Havana, Cuba, founded by Fidel Castro, to provide free education, room, and board for students from underdeveloped countries. Ten U.S.-based students who are committed to working in medically under-served communities in the U.S. graduated this year.

At the graduation ceremony, there was a passionate, enthusiast song and dance tribute to Fidel Castro ending with a "Viva Castro" and a raised clenched fist. There are revolutionary slogans on buildings and walls. When asked, most Cubans give a "I can't talk about it" look.

The Cubans I interacted with were friendly. It's a big and crowded city, though, where people do not make eye contact. I was told there are informers in every group. Soldiers walk in pairs and do not interact with their fellow citizens. Still, it felt like they were ignoring us as we walked down the street. A local said that we are ghosts to them—here today, gone tomorrow.

Five days later, I have a sense of Cuban time. If you order dinner, it might take an hour to appear. Things move slowly for two reasons, I believe. One, it is *very* hot and muggy. Two, there is little or no incentive to work hard. Every Cuban receives ten *cucs* a month (about $10). That's it. Cubans, therefore, find other ways to earn money, such as from tips while driving a taxi or leading a tour.

Cubans hang out watching the street from their balcony, or stand on the sidewalk, or talk to people through their metal window gate. The infrastructure has fallen apart, with totally stained and crumbling buildings and streets, garbage piling up, rusted railings on upper stories, with maybe a little store in the bottom room of a home. Every structure, except the blocky Russian buildings, had wrought iron railings, and in my mind's eye I could imagine how beautiful it must have looked in Hemmingway's day. Instead, I was told to walk in the middle of the street after a downpour so that crumbling balconies don't fall on you.

The landing back in Ft. Lauderdale elicited cheers and applause. Post-trip, I am left unsettled and changed, and I find it hard to put my thoughts into words. I look at things differently now and am grateful for much of what I once took for granted. My prayer, though, is that someday we narrow the gap between the wealthy and the poor.

My Growing Edge

SUSAN JOSEPHS

A vessel must empty before it can fill.

–Idries Shah

I am emptying in the most literal sense. Again. Clearing out old papers, and tossing clothes and objects, I reminisce over previous "selves." Even my iPhone contacts list is fair game. As I clear drawers, boxes, and file folders of education, metaphysics, and other workshops I've led, I'm confronted with the question, "Is this still me?" Partly, my decisions are sentimental. Why am I never able to simply toss the detritus?

As I review every sales slip my antique collector father-in-law had saved, I ruminate on the kind of man he was. He'd spent much of his time combing antique stores for treasures and *objets d'art*. My husband finds it hard to part with many of the possessions, despite the fact that they were often more important to his father than my husband was. Steve would follow his son around the house with a rag and carborundum, wiping his fingerprints off walls and objects. Neither the receipts nor the stuff gives me any deeper sense of who this enigmatic man was.

My dilemma is exaggerated by my hallucination that our children will want to go through our belongings, attempting to understand the parents they only thought they knew while rescuing items of our family history. Everything I read suggests this is not the case. That has not stopped me.

Moving, in 2013, from a home that had more storage capacity than the Smithsonian Institute, we schlepped 22,000 pounds of God knows what, to a house with much less room. We'd downsized considerably. I thought my purging was done with that move. But, six years later, I have yet to open packages, paintings, and boxes of tchotchkes. They must be very important.

While these activities appear mundane, symbolically, this emptying is different. A recent health scare, two strokes within six months, has increased my "level of concern," as educator Madeline Hunter used to say. The immediacy summons action. A sense of vulnerable merging overtakes my once more singular identity. Trying to be both practical and reflective, I'm settling into life's new pull. Discarding stuff feels like a metaphor for letting go in more metaphysical ways.

My edge is quite literally growing; my psychophysical boundaries are expanding, and I'm merging into an amorphic otherness. I'm motivated to "give up" the sense of self that once defined me. Not just ego, but habits of mind are challenged to transform. The light from the outer world entices less; the external noise is not so distracting. A shifted focus reorients me toward a more complacent engagement, not because of lack of interest or due to boredom, but to allow more discernment. But tears sometimes cascade at unexpected moments as I contemplate the unknown.

Mortality has become a motivator, a liberator, and a reconciler. Difficult to verbalize, my mentation is more fluid. I newly embrace casual acquaintances and groups whose goals I clearly share, without the passion or urgency of my former selves. It's not that I don't care, but my being is more defined by my assimilation with others than with the ego of old.

There is hint of a fresh understanding that awaits me if this vessel can acquire new capacity. I continue to empty. . .

Racist Ram

LAURIE LEINONEN

In afternoon calm
Wintry cheeks redden and blow
Melodies arrive

D ried pink roses sit in a jar on a windowsill along with three tea lights, three smooth grey stones, and one brightly colored card. Grey linen curtains frame small glass panes that look out upon a classically stark Vermont landscape with stands of tall, thin trees silhouetted against a snow-covered landscape. A new layer of snow thickens and bends a clothesline, weaving it into a linear tapestry of bare tree branches.

A harmonica is vibrating in the background, with surprising improvised melodies humming in and out as the young one learns to control his breathing to make musical sounds.

Now, "Clap, please," for the bowing of this bare-legged five-year-old, scantily dressed in colorful anime underwear.

Our little harmonica man plays on with increasing confidence. "Time to dance," he exclaims, as he carries on with his harmonica concert. His eyebrows go up and down in time with the emerging sounds, while his cheeks and face redden as he puffs in and out and blows and blows until he suddenly concludes his impromptu performance with a stately bow. Time for a break and a drink of water. Performing is exhilarating but also exhausting.

His pregnant mother asks to have her bulging baby bump wrapped and bound, encouraging the fetus within to get into a birthing position. She sips some wine, bounces on a balance ball, goes for a walk, stretches, bends, and massages her belly while hopefully awaiting an arrival sign, but this baby is happily and contentedly ensconced with his own magical timeline.

Farm Manager Gwynn joins us for dinner and recounts the story of a Racist Ram. She purchased this ram, with the assurance that he would be a good breeder. He appeared to be as frisky in the field as he was supposed to be. Later, when they checked the sheep for pregnancy, something unusual resulted. It seemed only the white sheep were pregnant.

Gwynn separated the impregnated ones, and suddenly the barn resembled the old Segregated South. There were white sheep in one section while the adjacent section held only Black. The vet came by to double-check the sheep. As she entered the barn, she recognized immediately the segregationist image and determined that this was, indeed, a Racist Ram.

In most of Vermont, racial and ethnic diversity are difficult to find, though socio-economic and educational divides are apparent. My daughter and her Egyptian husband are teachers at a small private, elite boarding school and organic farm. As most of the country is doing these days, they are addressing the history of institutional racism at the school. This semester, as a result of concerted efforts, more than twenty of forty-six students enrolled identify as students of color. Ideally, a positive and much-needed change.

The five-year-old illustrates and dictates a welcoming story book for the baby, who stretches within Momma's womb as he considers when to emerge into this turbulent time. Perhaps he and his older brother will be partners in making powerful music to enlighten the rest of the world.

Age Is Just a Number

PEGGY WALLIS

I have been sitting on the dune for ages, staring out at the ocean. The beach is littered with seaweed and tar. The blue and purple bodies of men of war, bubble-shaped jellyfish with intricate ridges that mimic a spine, send out unseen tentacles under the sandy surface and must be avoided. Tangled in a clump of seaweed, I see what looks like an insulin syringe. Light sparks at the edge of my eyesight turn into sunlight reflected off the ocean. After walking down the beach for hours, it feels good to rest. An emaciated woman lies on a towel just beyond my feet, deep brown in the sun. It is impossible to guess her age.

I am in Florida; salty, sandy, and hot. It is a yearly pilgrimage that I have been making since I was ten, and I spent my winter break with my grandparents in Miami. In those days, Miami's South Beach was a conglomeration of small, modest art deco hotels populated by elderly retirees escaping the Northeast's winter chill. As I watched them rocking away the days on their front porch, I vowed to never get old. And to never live in Florida.

I continued these visits throughout my high school and college vacations until, newly married and with young children, I began to visit my own retired parents in Florida. Living in a gated country club community was a far cry from the Miami of my childhood, which had changed dramatically. South Beach was now teeming with models, muscular young men showing off their physiques, and wealthy cocaine-addled visitors. The rocking chairs are gone, with their quiet front porches replaced by noisy upscale hotels. The ladies who rocked in the sun, unashamedly old, letting their gray hair curl wildly in the humidity, are also gone.

The retirees who now live in my parents' Florida, these grandparents of my children and their friends, play golf and tennis. The women are well-dieted and fanatically hunt down any hint of gray in their hair, exercise religiously, and are skilled in the use of cosmetics. Surgery is not unheard of.

My granddaughter has just turned ten and loves to visit her Florida relatives, including her ninety-seven-year-old great grandmother, who looks forward to her visits. Predictably, after a glass of vodka, happy and well-loved, she will often say, "Age is just a number." And it might be, if you have your health, enough money to live comfortably, and good insurance. On the other hand, my father, plagued by illness, died at age seventy and liked to warn me that "Getting old is not for sissies." And there's truth in that as well. Two sides of the same coin; two personal views of aging. As for me, I'm somewhere between them, grateful for my life and health, an optimistic realist, hiking each day until I can't.

To my granddaughter, Florida is an endless beach and a house with a swimming pool in the yard. The beach is covered with lovely shells, and the men of war are beautifully colored and interesting to look at. But I see the syringe in the seaweed, the sting in the tentacle, and I am grateful to be agile enough to jump over the threat. Until I can't.

Fauda

SUSAN JOSEPHS

A re we on vacation in a land we never knew existed? I don't know how we got here, or where on earth we even are. Did we pack correctly for the journey? What's the climate? How long will we remain here? What language is being spoken? Is there a lesson we're supposed to be learning? It all feels so completely foreign.

Fauda is the name of an Israeli drama on Netflix. *Fauda* is Hebrew, from the Arabic term, meaning chaos. *Fauda* perfectly describes how life feels during the crazy COVID-19 interruption. As I try to focus on more substantial issues, read better books, accomplish more practical projects, and write on more light-hearted topics, I'm pulled into the eddy of this chaotic moment. I simply bear witness.

The *fauda* of this disruption affects every aspect of my being. On the one hand, I'm back in the role of a 1950s housewife: cooking, cleaning, and feeling trapped and isolated. But, instead of pulling my cookbooks off the shelf, I look up recipes on my iPhone and watch YouTube instructions. It is 2020, and technology has re-envisioned the world! We can remain in virtual touch with family and friends on Zoom and House Party and keep hyperconnected to the outside noise.

We are simultaneously slowing down and speeding up.

The opportunity to escape is constant and tempting. There is an incessant barrage of invitations to watch virtual lectures, on Road Scholar, the Jaipur Literature Festival, the *New York Times*, take virtual Silver Sneakers classes, yoga, Tai Chi, attend the Metropolitan Museum of Art, Denver Art Museum, and Louvre Museum virtual tours. Channel surfing through television and phone apps, we find ourselves simultaneously fleeing to so many offerings that we can't keep the stories straight. Then there's Instagram, Facebook, WhatsApp, and Messenger. Old friends and family we haven't spoken to in decades reach out as though we're all about to disappear. The vying and pulling on our attention offers a dangerous distraction from the *fauda*.

In a pretense to normalcy, I attempt to keep a routine. But the routine no longer satisfies. It's difficult to remain inwardly focused when the seesaw pulls my attention into the outer unknown. Even solving Sudoku, tile, and crossword puzzles can't numb the mind to the global turbulence.

The planet feels at war with itself. In America, COVID-19, an invisible virus, is attacking many of us. Despite the risk to our own physical well-being, people are protesting in the streets, demanding an end to police brutality, racial injustice, and the old way of keeping invisible the racial disparity we have allowed since 1619, the date the first slave ship landed in Virginia.

For some of us, the isolation, the hunger for social interaction, and the physical touch appear to have heightened our own humanness. We witness our fellow citizens, murdered and victimized. Our democracy's survival now demands repairing our inept response to institutional racism. Many of us seek ways to contribute to a just and permanent solution. It is time.

For some, the reality of our entrapment, from COVID-19 restrictions and other issues, causes denial. There is an alarming clash.

Too many Americans, and others around the globe prefer to hide under the rock of magical thinking and their obsession with certainty. Others of us, pulling our heads out of the sand, seek science, reason, knowledge, and understanding.

I long for a real vacation. I yearn to eat exotic foods, delight in learning new customs, and exchange hugs and ideas with new people in foreign lands. But if we have to be imprisoned by this forced expedition, let some good come out of it. Let the *fauda* be replaced. Humanity, let's learn our lessons. Can knowledge, compassion, understanding, and love prevail? May we all find peace.

A Highway Runs Through It

SARAH MASSEY-WARREN

but,
if time could kneel, as a catcher
shifts to his knees when the pitch is wild.

—Alison Fairbrother

When my family visited my grandparents in Worcester way back when, Judith and I shared a bedroom. Porcelain mice moseyed across her dresser. Twelve years older, Judith must have resented this intrusion. I know she was miffed at my meddling with her mice. But a bond developed that lasted throughout our years together. A Thanksgiving trip to Ithaca, when she taught at Cornell and I was thirteen, found her gleefully letting me drive in a parking lot surrounded by snowbanks at 1:00 a.m. We shared lobster and wine in Maine, a room at a Modern Language Association conference, and the deep love of my great aunt Nita, another strong supporter of the family women.

Now it's October nineteenth; I can't believe I'm driving I-80 again. The highway unspools as time runs backward, even as I speed headlong at eighty-five miles an hour. The familiar prairie skews; wolf trees howl. Never again will I make the pilgrimage to my mother's house; never again will I travel to Bloomington to see Judith, who died exactly eleven months after my mother.

Last week, I drove with my younger brother to clear out Judith's house, whose contents I inherited. For four frantic days, I felt like Air Traffic Control, choosing furniture and art to ship to siblings, daughters, and Judith's former students turned colleagues. The breathtaking circular coffee table with its bronze patina surface, something Judith chose when I visited her some years back, I gave to Kathy, her friend and colleague, who devoted endless time and patience visiting Judith for the final months. I arranged for hospice care when I flew out in June; Kathy, her husband, Raymie, and I went out for dinner and drank glasses of wine late at night while Judith slept.

A Chancelor's Scholar in early modern literature at Indiana University (IU) married to Talbot Donaldson, an internationally known medievalist who was thirty years her senior, Judith kept an extensive collection of valuable books. Floor-to-ceiling bookshelves lined both guest bedrooms, converted into offices. The master bedroom walk-in closet morphed into a library. Books in the living room, books in the basement. No room at the inn unless you are written in Middle English. I donated the most valuable ones to the Lilly Library, IU's rare book collection, and offered some to Kathy and Raymie, both early modern faculty. Some I took. The rest I sold to a rare bookseller, who said, "Yeah, the Lilly beat us again," and spent three hours with his crew hauling it off.

Judith championed women in a university system that routinely discriminates against women and minorities—and won. Impeccable in wardrobe and logic, she fought the administration with a ferocity that carried over into my family who only valued males. She had my back. Only I among my siblings had built a relationship with her; still, she was generous with all of us in her will. Judith always did the right thing. My sister and I have vowed to carry her spirit forward.

My house vibrates with furniture and art from Judith and my mother. It's like rumble in the jungle—the elephant coffee table, the African giraffe chair, the oversized wicker insect atop an elegant dresser from Judith's house, where I wanted to put her now wooden mice until my cat, Elia, pounced, the lion bookends, the elephant planters, and the lion wall hanging, all accented by my mother's paintings and mine.

I miss them. If time could kneel, I would make *Masgouf*, the Iraqi national dish, for my mom, a forever foodie. If time could kneel, I would send $X + Y$, a book on gender inequality written by a witty mathematician who teaches at an art university, to Judith.

A landscape of tension splits and knits my family, and a highway runs through it. If time could kneel, I would return to I-80.

Puzzle without a Picture

LUELLEN RAMEY

A couple of weeks ago, I began working on a 1,000-piece puzzle. The puzzle was entitled *Feline Pharaoh* and had a picture on the box of a black cat wearing a large ankh around its neck. I began working the puzzle only to realize that the puzzle picture was not the same as the one on the box. Dang it! Wouldn't you think it would be the same? I had to give up on using the picture on the box as any kind of guide. I worked on it one piece at a time until it was complete.

My current life feels like that. I had an image, a picture, of how my daily life was going and how it would continue. COVID-19 shattered that picture, and now I live my life one day at a time, not knowing what the future will look like. The only thing I'm really planning ahead for is groceries, so that there is only one trip to the grocery store every two weeks. And I have some Zoom meetings scheduled on my calendar.

Early on during this stay-at-home mandate, I had a to-do list. I found that I was not accomplishing much of what I had on my list. I was not using my time to clean and organize my closets, clean out my office and file drawers, or even read the stack of books on my nightstand. I was finding that I needed to throw out the to-do list and honor what

I defaulted to do with my time. I needed to live my life a day at a time, piece by piece, without a picture. I've found that my need to go outside in nature is a near-daily necessity. This past week, I hiked more than twenty miles, reacquainting myself with Flatirons Vista, Eldorado Mountain, Sanitas Valley, Dakota Ridge, and Marshall Mesa. Hiking alone has been a meditation, going at my own pace, stopping to view rock climbers and birds.

I have found contentment in living life more as a "staycation." I've slept when I needed to sleep, often going to bed quite late and getting up late. I've paid attention to when I'm hungry rather than relying on the clock to tell me when to eat. I've noticed more closely what I'm hungry for—and yes, I still need dark chocolate and red wine!

I have a candle on my hall table and sit for twenty minutes daily in front of it, remembering and honoring the two friends I've lost in the past month and all those I didn't know personally. While I knew Diane to be alive and well and living in Ypsilanti, Michigan, I knew I could contact her at any time and pick up where we left off. And now, I'm struck by the fact that I will never see her or talk with her again. I value my friends more deeply and have contacted more of them lately. I especially try to reach out to those who are sheltering alone.

I'm grateful for Marc, my significant other, who comes almost every evening. We share any news of family and friends over a drink, then prepare a nice dinner. We are keenly aware that we are in the "high-risk" group and only go out for exercise and food. Marc does go back to his own home daily to do his work and projects.

Life is good, I'm living it day by day, not knowing what the emerging picture is. For now, I have good food, good shelter, good companionship, and good health. My gratitude is greater knowing that the future could bring something unexpected.

About the Contributors

Laura K. Deal is a writer, poet, and storyteller who also helps people understand their dreams. You can hear her stories online on the Story Podcast, YouTube, and BYU Radio's Appleseed show. She lives in Colorado with her spouse and two mismatched cats. Find out more about her at www.LauraDeal.com.

Marina Florian is a project manager at the University of Colorado in Boulder, Colorado. Although she received her master's degree in architecture, her first love is English literature and writing.

Janat Horowitz lives in Boulder, Colorado, and has been a white-water rafting guide, Aspen ski lift operator, and café owner. For thirty years, she has taught *Process Painting*, a therapeutic abstract art form. She lives with her husband and two dogs, which do lots of tricks—the dogs, not the husband.

Susan Josephs is an educator, consultant, curriculum developer, and mother, grandmother, and pet lover. A native New Yorker, she and her husband live in Boulder, Colorado. Her teacher and parent guides are available at Hoopoe Books, www.hoopoebooks.com. Her essay "More Choices For Wade" appears in *From Dubs to Marbles*.

Laurie Leinonen grew up at the base of the Cascade mountains outside Seattle and has lived in the shadow of the Boulder foothills since 1978. Both her children were born and raised in Colorado.

Richard Mansbach is retired and lives in Erie, Colorado. He was an educator, a leader of rites of passage weekends for teenage boys, and a manager and practitioner of restorative justice practices. He has written a historical novel based on the Mullan Road in 1862 and has been published as a guest columnist in the *Boulder Daily Camera*.

Sarah Massey-Warren has worked as a landscape architect and writer for businesses and nonprofits and is currently teaching writing (professional, Creative Nonfiction, and environmental). She loves the land, lyric, literature, and the intersection. Equally, she loves her daughters, now grown, her granddaughter, her succession of cats and dogs, and her garden. She has previously published her work in *Creative Nonfiction, Cream City Review, Architecture, Historic Preservation,* and other journals and venues.

Mary Ann Paliani retired in 1995 after working for twenty-seven years as the information services manager at the Rocky Flats Nuclear Weapons Facility in Golden, Colorado. In her postretirement years, she obtained an MS in Information Systems. She recently published a guest column in the *Boulder Daily Camera*.

Jeffrey Peacock was born in Florida in 1942. He graduated high school in Tokyo, Japan, in 1960. He served in the U.S. Army in Germany, and later in Vietnam. Jeffrey graduated from Columbia University in 1969 with a bachelor's degree in political science. He joined the American Foreign Service and served in Lebanon, Saudi Arabia, Italy, Greece, and Japan, retiring in 2002. He lives in Boulder, Colorado.

Luellen Ramey is Professor Emeritus, Department of Counseling, Oakland University (OU), Rochester, Michigan, where she was on the faculty for over thirty years. Luellen taught clinical courses in mental health counseling and served as chair of the department for thirteen years. Internationally, she was the founder of the collaboration between the Departments of Counseling at OU and the University of Botswana. Luellen has published in an array of journals in her field. More recently, she has appeared twice as a guest columnist in the *Boulder Daily Camera*. Luellen retired to Boulder, Colorado, where she facilitates bereavement groups for Tru Hospice.

Beth Shaw is retired and lives in Boulder, Colorado. She taught literature at the college level, including assignments in China and Togo, West Africa. She was an international student advisor for twenty years and has written for international education publications.

Peggy Wallis retired from the practice of law after thirty years at the Boulder County Attorney's Office representing Child Protective Services. She has lived in Boulder, Colorado, for over forty years, has served on the Community Corrections Board, and has been a volunteer ombudsman for the Boulder County Area on Aging. She also participates in the Restorative Justice Community Accountability Process and Circles of Support and Accountability. She has been a presenter at the Kempe Center for the Prevention and Treatment of Child Abuse and Neglect and the Colorado County Attorney's Conference.

Jack Williamson retired as a chaplain in the U.S. Air Force after twenty-four years of service. He co-authored the book, *Divorce: Six Ways* *to Get Through the Bad Times. . . for Good* with Mary Ann Salerno. He, along with Sarah Massey-Warren, piloted the first intergenerational writing course at the University of Colorado. He is the grateful grandfather of two remarkable grandsons, both college students.